PRAISE FOR

Hard Asks
made easy

"Laura empowers you to understand the superpowers you already have and how to take advantage of those strengths. I've seen her work with our senior leaders to our young professionals and they all walk away more confident with their asks."

MAURA REGAN

President, Licensing International

"Ask this hard question: What can I do to bring happiness and fulfillment into my life? Get this easy answer: Read *Hard Asks Made Easy*.

JONATHAN E. MITCHELL

Private investor, Philanthropist

"I used 'Laura's 5 Laws on Asking' and not only did I get the CEO position, I got the salary I wanted. What are you waiting for?"

SARAH LEONARD

CEO, Steamboat Springs Chamber

"Laura empowers us all to overcome our fears before those hard conversations that we need to so often have in life. I hope all my patients read *Hard Asks Made Easy* because the more questions they ask me, the better I can serve them."

ARMIN M. TEHRANY, MD
Founder, Manhattan Orthopedic Care and Precision Cut Productions

"Laura has taught me to ASK — to stand up for myself and stand firm. The skill of self-advocacy is priceless."

CAROLINE BAULIG
Twenty years old

"*Hard Asks Made Easy* beautifully encompasses principles that I employ in my Upper West Side, NYC practice to help individuals, couples, and families heal relationships at home, improve them in the workplace, and build bridges to the outside world."

PATTI GERMAN, ME.D., LMFT
Marriage and family therapist, NYC

"*Hard Asks Made Easy* has taught me to know my audience before skillfully delivering my ask which has made a world of difference for the success of my business. The skills I have gained from this book have also strengthened my partnership with patients. This is a MUST-READ!"

JOAN MONACO, MD, MS
Plastic and reconstructive surgeon, NYC

"In my working with people and their finances, as well as my role as one of the founding family members of the Ohr-O'Keefe Museum of Art, Laura's book has definitely taught me the Art of the Ask Conversation, so I can best serve my clients and museum supporters."

JUSTIN O'KEEFE, CLU, CHFC, CAP, LFD

CEO, and Founder, The Memorial Asset Protection Plan

"Laura is masterful at getting exactly what she wants. If you want to build the skills and confidence needed to get what *you* want, your first step is diving into *Hard Asks Made Easy.*"

JESSICA CUNNINGHAM AKOTO

CEO, KIPP Philadelphia Schools

"*Hard Asks Made Easy* reminds us how powerful asking can be. I love when my clients ask me the hard questions, it's the only way I can help them make their best financial decisions for themselves and their family."

RORRIE GREGORIO

Partner, Family office leader, National accounting firm

Hard Asks
made easy

Hard Asks
made easy

How to Get *Exactly* What You Want

Laura Fredricks, JD

Published by Advantage, Charleston, South Carolina.
Member of Advantage Media.

ADVANTAGE is a registered trademark, and the Advantage colophon is a trademark of Advantage Media Group, Inc.

Printed in the United States of America.

10 9 8 7 6 5 4 3 2 1

ISBN: 978-1-64225-707-6 (Paperback)
ISBN: 978-1-64225-706-9 (eBook)

LCCN: 2023905576

Cover design by Megan Elger.
Layout design by Matthew Morse.

This publication is designed to provide accurate and authoritative information in regard to the subject matter covered. It is sold with the understanding that the publisher is not engaged in rendering legal, accounting, or other professional services. If legal advice or other expert assistance is required, the services of a competent professional person should be sought.

Advantage Media helps busy entrepreneurs, CEOs, and leaders write and publish a book to grow their business and become the authority in their field. Advantage authors comprise an exclusive community of industry professionals, idea-makers, and thought leaders. Do you have a book idea or manuscript for consideration? We would love to hear from you at **AdvantageMedia.com**.

For anyone who has struggled with asking for something
that you really wanted. After you read this book,
I hope you now have the courage and the confidence
to make those hard asks.

May you never be held back from getting exactly what you deserve.

Contents

Acknowledgments

Did you ever know someone who just brings out the very best in you? Well, this person for me is Bonnie Hearn Hill, an acclaimed author and my writing coach. Bonnie brought out a new writing voice in me, one that will capture and hold your attention by learning through my stories as well as my step-by-step process how you can—and will—be a fantastic asker. I simply could not have written this book or shared so much of myself in these stories without Bonnie. I am grateful and ecstatic to have her in my life. Our writing adventures together have just begun! Watch us!

Finding the right publisher and editing team takes a lot of work, and when you make the right decision, you know that your book is positioned to be a bestseller. I made that right decision when I met DeVasha Lloyd, vice president of Forbes Books. When I told her that I wanted to write a book that would show people how they could make the really hard asks, the ones that were holding them back from having their best lives ever, she said the content would appeal to anyone of any age and was so excited to make this book happen for me. Always beaming that bright and beautiful smile, she stayed with me throughout the whole book process. Thank you, DeVasha. May we continue our journey to be long-lasting friends and colleagues.

When Stephen Larkin, editorial manager of Forbes Books, reads your manuscript for the first time and loves it, you dance on air. Thank you, Stephen and the entire team at Advantage Forbes Books; we are family now.

Looking back on all the life lessons I have had throughout my careers in law and philanthropy, I am so appreciative of every person who helped me get exactly where I am today.

This is especially true for all of you who contacted me throughout the years with your really hard asks. Thank you for trusting me to help you.

I send a very special thank-you to you, the reader. Thank you for taking the time to read this book. I know it will forever change the way you ask and the way you think about yourself, your relationships, and your quality of life. That was my goal all along. Remember, as I always say: "The quality of your life depends on the quality of the questions you ask yourself and others." My money is on you!

Introduction

"Can you give me more money?"

"Do you have time for me?"

"Do you love me?"

These are some of the most difficult questions you will ever ask—questions I've been helping people just like you ask for more than twenty years. Most people don't understand the psychology of asking, which is why it is so difficult to ask for (let alone receive) the things that are essential in your life. In my previous books on The Ask©, I touched on how you can make these types of asks. Now, in response to requests from readers and those I personally mentor, I am taking a deeper dive. In this book, you'll learn how to ask for the following:

- A substantial raise
- A promotion with a new job title and more money
- Flexible work hours and the ability to work from home
- A mentor to guide your career
- Recognition from your boss and your peers
- Validation of your worth
- Help from your children
- Respect when you speak

- Spirituality back in your life
- A return to good health
- Money you loaned to someone close to you
- Forgiveness
- Meaningful and lasting relationships
- The truth from someone who betrayed you
- And, yes, love

These are all very hard asks, and they have been holding you back from living your best life. I'm going to teach you secret techniques that can make each one easier. In this book, you will learn the following:

1. The formula for all your asks
2. Devils that lure you away from asking
3. Temptations that trap you from getting any answer
4. Types of askers—Which are you?
5. The laws of asking

This book will also reveal which superpowers you may already have, strengths that will give you the winning edge on all your asks.

Over the course of my work, raising a total of a billion-plus dollars, I learned the psychology of asking and turned those nos and maybes into yeses, yeses, and yeses. Now I'm sharing with you what took me all those years to learn.

Now let's get started so you can start making the hard asks and getting what you want and deserve.

CHAPTER 1

The *Ask*—You Always Had It in You

You've asked. You've always asked. You just might not have known it, or you might not have known how good you were at asking at a very early age. Back then, you were able to freely ask with absolutely no filter, no hesitation, no second-guessing the hardest questions you probably have ever asked in your life. You might have screamed while doing so or asked stubbornly or calmly. The point is that, at a very early stage in your life, you did it because it meant the world to you. It was your universe, and you had to have answers on the spot. Take, for example, this three-year-old girl.

She was propped up high on her fluffy pillows, all nice and comfortable, surrounded by her universe of white sheets. The days were long, and without being able to get out of bed or move around, she had to rely on her best two muscles—her eyes—and the land of her imagination. She had her best friend with her, SoJo, her sock monkey. Outlining the trim of that floor was a horizontal line of white lights, perfectly spaced about three inches apart. She waited for them to turn on and off, which they did when it was time for the people to go. Then tremendous sadness and loneliness set in.

Every day, her mother would come to her bedside with handmade cards from children at St. Matthews, the school she was going to attend in a few years. Most of messages were written vertically, as if the last word had to fly off the card and touch the sky. St. Matthews had a lot of work to do if these children were ever going to learn to write in straight lines.

The nurses at the hospital always seemed to be busy every moment of the day, taking temperatures, reading charts, and talking to the children and their families. They were everywhere. Later, when she was of school age, she came to learn the intense similarities of nurses and nuns. They both had the same mission: to torture you while they tell you it is for your own good. Both had tests, many tests, to take—whether it involved your pulse, your heart rate, or spelling or math quizzes. Both always had the upper hand because they were the experts, the guardians guiding your health or education. You could never answer back or disagree. Both were eager to tell your parents about everything you did wrong or how you simply would not cooperate. They always said it with fake smiles.

Every evening at exactly eight o'clock, the horizontal line of white lights on the floor would flash on and off for two minutes. It was time for all visitors to leave. That's when it got quiet, very quiet, and the children would start crying. It only took one to start, and all the rest felt the pain and began to join in. It was like a crying chorus, and the weight of the sounds changed everyone's moods. It was at that moment the questions began:

- "Why didn't Daddy come?"
- "When will he ever come?"

- "Why can't I go home now?"
- "How much longer will I be here?"
- "Can't you stay longer?"
- "Am I going to be able to play again?"
- "Will I be able to walk again?"

That girl was me. And that was when I learned to ask.

You, too, learned to ask at a very young age. You always had that power, that desire, to have answers that would fulfill you as a person. *You always asked without knowing you were asking.* Would it not be amazing if we could go back in time and return to those innocent and simple days when getting the answer to just one or two questions would make your day, and nothing else in the world mattered?

Whether you were three years old, younger, or a few years older, you asked from your heart, from your soul, from your being, and the words just came out. You might have screamed while doing so or asked stubbornly or calmly. The point is that at a very early stage in your life, you did it because it meant the world to you. It was your universe, and you had to have answers on the spot.

> You always had that power, that desire, to have answers that would fulfill you as a person. You always asked without knowing you were asking.

This book begins at just that moment in time in your life because it is important for you to remember that you always had that power, that desire, to have answers that would fulfill you as a person. *You always asked without knowing you were asking.*

As we grow older from childhood, through adulthood, responsibilities, life experiences, hardships, challenges, personal achievements, and victories become the silent backdrops when we want to ask. We can easily recall incidents when we were about to ask for something,

7

and the floodgate of emotions and past experiences and reactions caused us to stop. I have heard people say that they stopped before asking because the other person would

- stop liking them,
- stop loving them,
- think they were a bank or ATM,
- ask them to go to someone else,
- judge them,
- avoid them,
- send them to a different person,
- write them off,
- think they were inadequate, or
- think they were immature.

I've asked them why they felt this way, and it is always based on a "past" experience. In the past when they did ask, they usually experience one of these reactions:

- They were ignored.
- They were stared down.
- They were laughed at.
- They were patronized.
- They were brushed off.
- They were intimidated.

This is a terrible way to live—unfulfilled because you could not ask for something that you really wanted or, worse, didn't ask for to avoid pain. Fear of rejection and fear of hearing a "no" to your ask has always prevented many people from asking. It is so understandable that you would want to avoid pain by not asking. However, feeling patronized, intimidated, or ignored after an ask has been made is just as unacceptable and certainly is no way to live a life. Sadly, it just takes one or two instances when an ask has been made and met with these types of rejections to prevent many people from ever asking again.

An exercise for you is to dig deep, really deep. When can you recall asking really hard questions? What were they? What answers and reactions did you receive? What did you do, and what was your reaction? More importantly, how did you feel? Did these experiences shape how you grew up in your teens, young adult, and adult life? Did they guide how you raised or mentored your children, grandchildren, nieces, nephews, colleagues, or friends? If you think this exercise is not worth your time, or that it only has a miniscule effect on how it shaped your life, consider the story about Jane Goodall, the English primatologist and anthropologist.

Goodall learned at the age of four that asking an important question at an early age would shape the course of her future career. She's written the children's book *The Story of How a Hen Lays an Egg*. In her blog, *Jane Says*, she writes about how her curious determination and one question paved the way for her prolific career: she wanted to know how, on a chicken, there was an opening big enough for an egg to come out, so she decided to observe by hiding under the henhouse.[1]

Goodall went on to become the founder of the Jane Goodall Institute and the Roots & Shoots program and has worked extensively on conservation and animal welfare issues. She was named a UN Messenger of Peace and is a member of the World Future Council.

I purposely began this book with these two anecdotes to show you that we can bring out the asker in you that you had all along in childhood. Through this simple yet powerful journey of recalling your memories of childhood, when you asked with abandon, I hope you

1   Jane Goodall, "The Story of How a Hen Lays an Egg," Jane Goodall's Good for All News, May 2016, accessed February 15, 2023, https://news.janegoodall.org/2016/05/04/story-hen-lays-egg.

see now that you are merely dusting off a skill you have always had. It's there; we just need to bring it out and make some refinements. When I remind people that they really were great askers at a young age, I often receive a reaction of "Oh yeah, you're right." This is exactly the place where I want to begin with you. You have the asking skills in you. Now let's put them to work in your life, whatever your age.

Trust Your Instincts

One of my favorite mantras is this: "When I don't trust my instinct, I lose." I do believe that each of us has that small intuitive voice that goes off in our heads when asks and decisions need to be made. I've put this to the test many times, particularly early in my career, when I was applying for a job, and then later, when people would ask me to help guide them with their job searches. The voice that only you can hear gives you the signs, the clues, that something is going well and, more importantly, that you really want this opportunity. For instance, while I was living in New York City, I interviewed for the top fundraising position at a large foundation that was located outside of NYC. The person who headed the search committee asked me questions about how I transitioned out of law (some thirty years before) and how could I possibly come to an area where I didn't know anyone and raise money. He wasn't asking me how I would approach raising money in the current economic environment, what techniques had been most successful and would be for their organization, or what my management style was. He also wasn't listening when I said I moved to Philadelphia not knowing anyone, helped raise $300 million, and then moved to NYC not knowing anyone and raised $100 million right after 9/11. Or that during my consulting career, each client was in a new state where I knew no one, yet each client's fundraising program soared. During the interview I hearkened back to another phrase I created and rely on often, which is "How they treat the process is how you will be treated." My instinct told me not to ask for this job because it was not a good fit for me. Just look at the way we were getting started; it was a total disconnect. If I did had listened to my instinct, I would have lost, meaning that I would have been stuck in a job that simply was not right for me.

You may be curious that I used the phrase "Ask for the job" in the above example. After all, during the job-seeking process, you send your résumé, and then if they like you on paper, they interview you, and then they decide whether or not to make you an offer. Here is a real eye-opener for you. When you ask for the job, you have a much better chance of getting the job. This bears repeating: when you ask for the job, you have a much better chance of getting the job.

I have a friend (let's call him Leon) who is a rising actor here in NYC. He auditions for parts he calls being the "bad guy," one who is a foreign character in the script or speaks a different language from the rest of the characters in the movie or series. Leon's physique lends itself perfectly for these types of parts because he is tall, very thin, and physically fit. He can disguise himself under a beard or really bad stubble on his face.

> When you ask for the job, you have a much better chance of getting the job.

Leon asked me why, after he always came so close to getting a part, he lost out to someone else. After listening to what transpired during his most recent auditions, I asked, "At the end of the audition, did you ask for the part, Leon?"

"No." He looked confused as to why he should because he was auditioning, so naturally they knew he wanted it.

"When you ask for the part," I said, "you are demonstrating that you are committed to the success of the film or series and that you want to be part of its success. You have declared that no one else is better than you for the part."

While Leon still looked a bit confused, he knew these prior parts were perfect for him. His intuition and gut had told him so. He then asked me what words he should he use to ask for the part at his next audition.

I suggested that he use his own tone of voice with laser eye focus and say, "I feel so at home with this part, and I am committed to the overall success of the film/series. Thank you for the opportunity to learn from you and to have the chance to show you my talent and my commitment. I'm asking you now: Will you select me for the part?"

It sounds awkward at first, I know, but here's what happened. Not only did Leon get that part, but also he went on to get reoccurring parts on *The Blacklist* and *Law and Order: Organized Crime*. Now do you see the power of asking for the job?

Whenever you have that initial thought that you'd like to ask for something—whether it is for a new acting role, for a new job, or for someone to help you do something—recognize that your inner instinct kicks in, which can guide you during your ask. There is that tendency to push our intuition down with the rationalization that we should be taking a more mature and responsible approach. We will go into great detail about how to handle really hard asks in chapter 9, yet it is worth pointing out here how important it is to trust your instinct during the ask process. I believe and have heard from many people that one of the hardest asks anyone can make is to ask for help. When you do that, your request can make people feel helpless, out of control, less than, or irresponsible. We have the tendency to judge ourselves by looking around and seeing and hearing other people coping with life just fine without asking for help.

What I would like you to do the next time you know you need to ask for help—say, to have a parent pick up your child from soccer practice, or a sibling who can make the summer vacation plans instead of you because you just received a large work project, or a friend to make a phone call to a colleague who may be able to recommend an investor or two for your new venture, or a friend to work out with you so that you keep on your exercise regimen—is to listen to that voice in your head, your instinct. What is it telling you? If it feels right, then make your ask. If it doesn't, then take a moment to yourself and ask why. What is coming up for you? Do you think the person you're asking won't like you? Think less of you? Turn you down or, worse, mock you because you should be able to do it yourself? Or (and think carefully on this one) how badly do you want it—and do you deserve it?

Most asks for help are not made because we rationalize that we may think we deserve them, but when we keep talking inside our heads, we talk ourselves out of believing we deserve them. We also think that we should be that better person and juggle it all. Take a few minutes and listen to your true instinct, the stronger voice that will guide you to ask or not ask. When we talk about instinct, it is the voice that you and you alone hear. Don't ignore it. Work with it, and then you'll know exactly how important it is for you to ask. Remember Leon. He got the part and many more parts after he not only knew these roles were right for him but also actually asked for them.

Tackle the Two Devils

I was doing a session for a wonderful group of professional women—smart, savvy, astute business leaders and entrepreneurs who mainly came to hear how they could ask their current client and customer bases for more contracts and more orders. I learn so much from these sessions, and my biggest learning moment has always been for me to ask good questions first and then work through the issues with the audience.

One woman was the lead project manager for a large construction company. She asked me why she always had to "chase" after her top clients, with whom she has had a close and ongoing relationship,

Expectation is our first devil when it comes to making an ask.

for more business each year. She said her company generously invites these clients to annual sporting events and cocktail receptions with prominent thought leaders as the guest speakers. Furthermore, the company always sends a gift to the clients' employees during the holidays. I asked her one simple question: "Why do you feel these clients owe you more business?"

Her response drives at the heart of our first devil: "Because we've done so much for them … shouldn't they know we want their repeat business?" There you have it—expectation. Expectation is our first devil when it comes to making an ask. It could apply to many situations when you expect the person receiving your time and attention to know what you want. You might expect that picking up an extra project at work will automatically be remembered by your boss when you discuss your upcoming bonus. You might expect that giving your child a certain look will remind him to play nicely with his sister. You may expect that when you have told a good friend that you are free to help them after their surgery, you will be the first one they call when they are in need of help. When you catch yourself saying things and doing things that indicate you expect the other person will know exactly what you mean and will do what you anticipate, take a minute and see if you actually asked for what you wanted. Chances are you never asked.

In the example of our project manager, she looked back and saw all her effort, her outreach, and her activity with her top clients, but the one thing she missed was that she never asked them for more business. She expected it. You can dodge the first devil that can sabotage your efforts by making sure you ask, not expect.

This leads us right into our second devil: assumption. Before we ask, or when we never get the words out to ask, we have the tendency to make a lot of assumptions. I see this taking place many times in personal relationships. For example, let's say a couple who's been dating for a while decides to live together in the same apartment. During the discussion of how and when they make the move to live together, finances come up. They decide to split all expenses evenly, and that includes when they go out to dinner alone or with friends. Once they are all settled in, our happy couple decides to go out for dinner a few times over the course of a month. But with each dinner, only one of them consistently picks up the check. Here's where assumptions come to the fronts of our minds. Assumptions go both ways when specific asks are not made. There are assumptions on the part of the person who should have asked and assumptions on the part of the person who was never asked. They sound like this:

- "Next time she'll pick up the check."
- "He said he had to buy some things for his mother this month; I'm sure that's the reason why he's not paying."

- "I paid for the groceries and our last heating bill, so he should pay this dinner bill to make it even."
- "I'm pretty sure I paid for dinner the last time or two, so this time it's her turn."

Do any of these thoughts sound familiar to you? Unfortunately, assumptions are the seeds we sow that grow into future arguments. Inevitably the person in this couple who is continuing to pay for dinner when the agreement was that all expenses would be split is going to raise the issue and probably cause an argument. All this tension can easily be resolved by an ask. It takes practice, for sure, but it would have been better in this situation if the person paying for dinner a number of times said something like this:

"I am happy we had the chance to have dinner together and get away for a bit. I do believe we agreed a while ago that we would split the cost of dinner, and you may be unaware, but I have paid the last few times. Going forward, is this still the arrangement we want? And if so, how do we let each other know when it is their turn to treat for dinner?"

Push Away the Three Temptations

When you are at the point of thinking that you should ask, there are three temptations that lure you away from verbally making your ask:

1. Luck
2. Chance
3. Time

I put these three tempters together because they tend to overlap with each other. There is a tendency—a real human tendency—to rely on all three of these. We can be lucky on our own scorecard of getting things that we want personally and professionally without ever asking.

We can hedge our bets that we will get what we want because luck is on our side, and life is going pretty well right now. We can just let time takes its course, and down the road, we will get what we want. While all three can jeopardize your ability to get exactly what you want quickly, I think that time is the biggest culprit here. Let me illustrate.

There was a financial and philanthropic planner who came with his colleagues to a local chamber of commerce meeting where I was speaking. After I covered Laura's Five Laws of Asking, which I'll share in chapters 4 through 8, he raised his hand and said, "Three times a year, I play golf with my top clients. They know why I am doing this, and I know in time I will gain their business to invest with me." I could see he felt very proud to stand up in the crowd and make this statement, but I also sensed it was a challenge that my five laws seemed like a lot of unnecessary work for him and his colleagues. I have to admit, I love a good challenge, and it is the lawyer in me that wanted to immediately get into a lively debate. The better side of me came out with measured patience and my renewed commitment to active listening. "And how is this all working out for you to date?" I asked him.

He looked down and said, "It's coming along."

At this point, I could not contain my directness because I really wanted him to get the business sooner rather than waiting on his luck, thinking that a time period would lead this prospective client to him.

"Why don't you simply say to him that it would be invaluable to you and your firm if he would consider trusting you with his investments?" I asked. He looked at me and said nothing. I then continued, "Why don't you want to ask him?"

And here it is! He said, "Because I don't want to hear no or that he's investing with someone else."

Go over this example very carefully. Do you see where the assumptions came in without even a conversation? Our reluctant financial and philanthropic advisor was assuming that if he did ask, he would either hear, "No" or hear that this potential client would consider someone else and not him. At the end of the session, I went up to him privately and, with much sincerity, thanked him for his honesty. I said that I really thought things would go much better if he spoke from his heart, backed by his expertise, and called this potential client and asked him for his business. He smiled and said he would try.

Three weeks later, I received a surprise thank-you note. Our financial and philanthropic advisor did muster the courage to ask, and he got that potential client's business. I was thrilled because my happiness comes from success stories like this one. I know it took a lot for him to make this ask, and honestly I have no idea what words he used, but he asked, and now we have a happy client and a happy financial and philanthropic investor.

Now it's your turn. When you find yourself in a position in which you have not asked but need to, are you relying too heavily on luck, chance, or time? Push those temptations away, and make your ask.

Now that we know what may be holding you back from making your ask and what we all need to do to push away our devils and tempters, it's time to find out what type of asker you are. You may fit into one category or several, but it is important to know your asking style so that going forward, you can fully embrace the ask techniques I'm about to give you. If you know your baseline, you will know where you need to go. There is no right asker, and there is no wrong asker. Read the advantages, challenges, and refinements that follow with each type so that you can fully embrace, absorb, and know how to use the information I'm about to share with you.

Takeaways

- At a young age, you asked incredibly hard questions without fear or hesitation, and with conviction. The ask has always been in you.
- Trust your instincts because they will be your inner strength with each ask you make.
- The two devils—expectations and assumptions—can sabotage your asks. Keep them in check, and be sure that these two devils are not preventing you from asking.
- The three tempters—luck, chance, and time—can postpone or prevent you from making your ask. Make sure you are not relying on any one of these as a crutch for not asking.

CHAPTER 2

The Four Asking Types— Which Are You?

DeVasha likes to be strategic and negotiate her asks while making everyone feel at home. Dom likes to be more direct and let you know right up front his business dream and how you can be a part of his business. How about you? When you ask, what is your style? Over the past several decades of coaching and training people on how they can enhance their lives with the right asks—and raising a lot of money making the right asks along the way—I discovered there are really only four asking types. These types are organic representations of how we all ask in life. So with the knowledge and experience I have had raising money and helping people nationally and internationally get their best lives through the ask, I have identified the four askers.

I did it so you would know and have as a baseline the type of asker you are. When I asked my friend Tess why she'd like to know the type she is, she summed it up perfectly: "I need to understand myself so that I can move forward."

Knowing initially the type you are like is a two-sided coin. You will learn how your type helps you personally and professionally as well as how it could possibly be holding you back from the opportunities you most desire. I will first give a broad overview of the four asking types to give you an idea of what those types may look and sound like. This is a generalization of the four types, and we will get into much more detail after you take the four asking types quiz. As you read the descriptions, please don't get caught up in feeling that you may not be this type because it is "male" or "female." Pay attention to their descriptive personality, body language, how they dress, and what their asks may sound like.

Before you take the quiz, you need to do a short exercise. Think back on when you had to ask for something at work—say, asking for an extension of time to complete a project, asking for the help of a coworker to finish an upcoming presentation on time, or asking your boss for a raise, promotion, or new job title or for you to work from home. Think back on when you had to ask a friend to be there for you while you were going through a stressful time, or your partner to pay more attention to you, or your parents to stop arguing with you, or your children to start paying for their own expenses. Put yourself in a moment similar to these, and then take the quiz. Please be open and honest. There are no "good" types or "terrible" types. You may find yourself in one or more types, which is quite common. The purpose of this exercise is to find out your asking type right now. With each type, there are ways to make improvements and refinements. Refinements will be in the words you select as well as the body language you may be showing when you ask. Once we establish these refinements, you will be able to see how you can use them to fully absorb the ask tips, techniques, and exercises contained in chapters that follow.

The purpose of finding out how you come across now when you ask is so that going forward, you can learn how to make subtle changes to your asking style to get the best results with each ask you make.

Now it is time to take the quiz, either in this book below or on my website, www.ExpertonTheAsk.com.

Overview of the Four Asking Types

DeVasha is a soft-spoken, strategic, always smiling person. She's an impeccable dresser, and if you ever did a video meeting with her, you could see in her background that her home office looks like something out of *Architectural Digest*. She never interrupts when someone is speaking. In fact, when others speak, you can see in her eyes that she is quietly thinking of what her next response should be. You may have heard it is a negative, but in truth, it is a highly effective tactic that you can perfect. If it appears to her that someone is dominating the conversation, she quietly restores the balance. When it is time to ask, her negotiation skills are in full focus. She has her eyes on the prize to get to yes, and she strategically suggests ways to make that happen. Her ask might sound something like this: "I think you agree we are at the point to sign the contract. Anything else?"

Tyler is a deep thinker and an even deeper listener. He lets the person he is asking speak about themselves before he speaks. Since Tyler has a wonderful sympathetic ear, during the ask, many people take the liberty of unloading their complaints or problems to him. He is always patient, kind, and understanding with each person. His clothing style has a relaxed and comfortable feel that reflects Tyler's relaxed and comfortable style. When Tyler asks, he likes to put himself in the shoes of the person being asked, anticipating how they may feel or react to his ask. Tyler's ask might sound something like this: "I know how busy you are with your new position at work, but would it all be possible for you to speak as an author at our book club next month?"

Kai is a human magnet. When she walks into a room, everyone wants to be around her. She works hard on fostering strong, close relationships with everyone in her network. She has earned the admiration and respect from the leaders in her industry. Her winning combination of intellect, ingenuity, and humor draws people in, making them want to hear more about what she has to share. All her conversations are convincing and compelling. She selects a trendy piece of clothing or an accessory that always spurs a good conversation with her friends and peers. Kai rarely has to ask because she relies on her strong connections, her solid relationships with people, and her conversant style. She knows they will do the right thing to help if she needs something, all in good time. If she did have to ask, it may sound something like this: "I'm so happy to have this time to explain the parameters and scope of the project to build our new $5 million community center. This will be the focal point of our city, where everyone of all ages will have a place to enjoy recreation, arts, education, and wellness. It will attract new home buyers and make our existing community even stronger. Funding will come from tax credits and loans, and of course we'd love for you and your company to be a large part of our success."

Dom, in a word, is charismatic. His passion, conviction, and focus on achieving his goals is what motivates him every day. He will walk right up to you with a big grin, introduce himself, and say what he wants. When he shares a story about his background or his current work, his honesty wins you over, even if the delivery of the story may at times be very direct. His clothing style is contemporary, but it does not outshine his captivating conversation. Dom's ask may sound like this: "My mission is to fix one hundred bicycles a year and to give them to anyone who needs one for transportation or pleasure. I'm looking for people like you who can contribute $250 this Christmas to give a child or an adult in need a new bike. Here's my card."

Quiz Time

Now that you've seen the overview about the four asking types, it's time for you to find out which one or ones you are. You can take the quiz below or online: www.ExpertonTheAsk.com. Remember that honesty wins the day. This is just the launching point for you to know your style so that you can implement immediately the practical asking advice—particularly Laura's Five Laws of Asking—that you will learn in the following chapters. This quiz can be particularly helpful for you professionally if you work in industries where asks are made for sales, charitable gifts, renewed and expanded contracts, new hires, new business, training programs, and investments. The quiz will also help you to recognize how you ask now, and with some tweaks, will enhance your asking style to help you reach your goals faster. The quiz can be equally helpful for you in all your personal relationships because you will recognize how you have been asking for some support, love, forgiveness, or spiritual guidance and help. With the help of this book, you will have the tools going forward to make these emotional asks with confidence and with ease.

The Four Asking Types Quiz

With each question, select just one that best fits how you ask right now. Select or circle the number that accompanies your selection. At the end of the quiz, see which number you have selected the most.

That will be your asking style. The second-most-selected number will be the secondary asking style that blends with your dominant asking style. Here we go:

I like to negotiate during the ask.	1
I negotiate sometimes when I ask.	3
I wait to see the person's response when I ask, then I negotiate.	2
I never negotiate when I ask.	4

My personality helps me to get a yes answer.	4
My relationships with people help me to get a yes answer.	3
When I ask, my honesty will get us to a yes answer.	2
If I am strategic when I ask, it helps me to get a yes answer.	1

If I want someone special to do something for me, I do something first for them.	2
If I want someone special to do something for me, I ask them right away.	4
If I want someone special to do something for me, I think about it for a while and then ask them.	1
If I want someone special to do something for me, I pick the right time, I look my best, I bring on my positive attitude, and I know it will happen.	3

When I ask, getting a yes is the most important thing.	4
When I ask, making sure the other person is not offended or upset with me is the most important thing.	2
When I ask, maintaining my close relationship with the person is the most important thing.	3
When I ask, it is important that I ask in a strategic and thoughtful way.	1

When I ask someone close to me for help, I know they will just do the right thing.	3
When I ask someone close to me for help, I assume they will say yes.	4
When I ask someone close to me for help, I ask them what I can do for them.	2
When I ask someone close to me for help, I anticipate they will want to know all the details.	1

I ask when I have a strategic, well-thought-out plan.	1
I ask because I'm good at it.	4
I ask, even though I hate to hear a "no."	2
I ask because I've put the time into the relationship with the person I'm about to ask.	3

When someone gives me a "no" answer, I move on.	4
When someone gives me a "no" answer, I ask why.	1
When someone gives me a "no" answer, I ask them to stay friends/colleagues.	3
When someone gives me a "no" answer, I thank them and make sure they were not upset or caught off guard with my ask.	2

Results

- 1—You are the Negotiator.
- 2—You are the Emphasizer.
- 3—You are the Presenter.
- 4—You are the Charmer.

Type 1: The Negotiator

The Negotiator, like DeVasha, is someone who deeply desires to get to yes while, at the same time, making sure that everyone is at ease before, during, and after the ask. Their ask is important, and they would like everyone at the end of the negotiation to feel that they have won. No one should be pressured or slighted. The Negotiator often has a low, soothing, reassuring tone of voice. Should a rough topic arise, a surprise element to the conversation, the Negotiator is quick to smooth things over. The Negotiator likes to have the upper hand and does not like confrontation or unexpected challenges to tarnish or sidetrack the ask. This is why they often are impeccably dressed so that every detail, from their appearance to the selection of their words, is well planned out to avoid the unexpected. The Negotiator's body language demonstrates a great deal of nodding with the head in a "yes" motion, with the person smiling and leaning forward. The Negotiator often uses the following words and phrases during the ask:

- "Wouldn't you agree?"
- "I think we all are on the same page."
- "Good point."
- "Let us think about this a bit."

Advantages for the Negotiator

The pluses to being this type of asker is that, from the perspective of the person being asked, it is really nice to have a person put in so much time and give such detailed attention to the ask. Also, if the ask is done in a calm manner, the person being asked may be more apt to share more of themselves, which gives the Negotiator a tremendous advantage to get to a yes answer.

Challenges for the Negotiator

The challenges for the Negotiator are that this person may be going too overboard, concentrating and focusing on ensuring that everything goes smoothly. It may give the person being asked the impression that there is no urgency to make a decision. Hence, the Negotiator may have to spend more time circling back after the ask with phone calls, text messages, and meetings to get a definitive answer. Also, the Negotiator's body language may work against them if they are nodding too much or leaning in too much. The person being asked may feel that they have the upper hand with all these positive physical indicators during the ask, which may throw off the Negotiator's ask strategy.

Refinements for the Negotiator

1. Try weaving in stronger and more direct words when speaking with the person you are asking. Instead of saying, "I think you agree we are at the point to sign the contract; anything else?" say, "I believe we covered all the questions you had with the contract, and we are ready to move forward." This will help bring your ask to a quicker closer.

2. Be careful not to nod in a "yes" fashion and smile too much. It may come off the wrong way with the person you are asking. They may think they will be getting all they want in the ask. Additionally, they may feel your ask is not that important, or that if they say no, it will be just fine with you. Lessen the number of times you smile, and try looking at them directly without nodding "yes" too much.

3. If a controversy, misunderstanding, or an unexpected discussion arises during the ask, instead of trying to smooth things over, address it in a calm tone. You might say: "I want to work through this with you right now. Can you explain a bit more about that last point you raised?"

Type 2: The Empathizer

The Empathizer, like Tyler, has one role, and that is to stand in the shoes of the person they are asking. The Empathizer internalizes what they would think and feel if they were asked for the same thing. This person has a big heart, and through their magnificent listening skills, they have the ability to understand how the person is going to feel and react when asked. During the asking process, the person they are asking generally is doing most of the talking. That is acknowledged with an occasional nod of the head by the Empathizer with very little additional body language. The Empathizer often uses the following words and phrases during the ask:

- "How wonderful for you."
- "I totally understand."
- "I know exactly what you are saying/thinking/feeling."
- "I'm sure this is very difficult for you."

Advantages for the Emphasizer

A plus to being this type of asker is just that: your empathetic approach. You genuinely care about each and every person you ask. You take the time to feel and sense how they will feel when they are asked. Your intuition and your insights into their lives make them feel at home and feel that they are liked and often loved by you and the organization or industry you represent.

Challenges for the Empathizer

The biggest challenge for the Empathizer is that you lose yourself when you ask. It is fine to appreciate and understand how someone will feel when you make your ask, but if you genuinely care about what you are about to ask for, you need to step back into your own shoes when you ask. Also, your conversation may be too one sided, with the person doing all the talking and you doing all the listening. This may actually take up all your time in your ask meeting, and you may not have the time left over to actually make your ask.

Refinements for the Empathizer

1. If you are making a professional ask, remember that *you are asking on behalf of the organization or institution. You are not asking for yourself.* This may help you keep a healthy distance between the person you are asking without alienating them.

2. If you are making a personal ask, reflect on this: At the moment of the ask, do you honestly believe in what you are asking for? If you do, you will stay in your shoes, not the ones of the person you are asking.

> If you are making a professional ask, remember that you are asking on behalf of the organization or institution. You are not asking for yourself.

3. Try changing and mixing up the words you select when you ask. Instead of saying, "I know how busy you are with your new position at work, but would it all be possible for you as an author to speak at our book club next month?" say, "This book club attracts top author speakers like you. We would be so honored if you would be our speaker next month at our book club. Will you do this for us?"

Type 3: The Presenter

The Presenter, like Kai, draws her asking power through her presence, her strong relationships, and her captivating conversations. When the Presenter enters the room, you know it, and you feel it, and when they speak, they are funny and smart, and they always have something interesting to share. Their clothing selection is well thought out. A pin, signature cufflink, pocket square, or other eye-catching accent piece always invites a conversation, which is why they chose to wear it. The Presenter has worked hard on maintaining strong, close personal relationships and even harder on forging new ones. The Presenter relies on the hard work put into those relationships to have those people come through when needed. Hence, asking is actually contained in the conversation and rarely directly ever made. The Presenter often uses the following words and phrases during the ask:

- "Don't you just love it when everything works out the way it should?"
- "This is terrific."
- "Of course I had you in mind."
- "I couldn't be happier."
- "Let's keep talking about this and meet after work next week."

Advantages for the Presenter

Their confidence and presence make you want to hear what they have to say, and that is a wonderful entry to any ask. The Presenter knows that it takes hard work and dedication to foster and maintain strong, binding work and personal relationships. They genuinely love to meet people, connect with people, and share what they know as well as learn from others. Their approach never comes across as fake or forced. The Presenter just loves to connect the dots in all conversations so that they can advance their agendas in good time.

Challenges for the Presenter

The biggest challenge for the Presenter is that they rely so heavily on the work that they put into creating these solid relationships that their ask may not come across as an ask at all. They have a tendency to weave the ask into the conversation and not make it stand out. The person they are asking may get lost in the conversation and may not hear or may not know that they were asked.

Refinements for the Presenter

1. Try to keep your conversations to this formula: you speak 25 percent of the time; they speak 75 percent. Later in the book, you'll see why this formula is so important when you ask. If you do most or all of the talking, your ask is not the focal point of your conversation, and you will wind up disappointed or confused as to why the person is not taking action on something you just talked about.

2. Make sure your magnetic personality as well as your standout clothing and accent pieces do not overwhelm or dominate the conversation time you need to prepare and deliver your ask. You need attention and focus on your ask if you want people to know you are asking them.

3. Shorten the wording of your ask, and be sure your ask is not hidden or buried in a multitude of facts and figures. You may be inclined to say this: "I'm so happy to have this time to explain the parameters and scope of the project to build our new $5 million community center. This will be the focal point for our city, where everyone of all ages will have a place to enjoy recreation, arts, education, and wellness. It will attract new home buyers and make our existing community even stronger. Funding will come from tax credits and loans, and of course we'd love for you and your company to be a large part of our success." Instead, though, you should say the following: "As we have been discussing, this $5 million community center project will play a big part in our community's future. Can I talk to you now about how you and your company can take a pivotal role to make this a success?"

Type 4: The Charmer

The Charmer, like Dom, knows just how to make an approach and knows just what to say to captivate an audience of one or an audience of many. Witty, likable, and driven, the Charmer has a mission, and that is to share the story about where they have come from and where they are now. Their goal is to convince you that you should get involved with their ventures and that not to do so would be a loss for you. They do have your best interests in mind, which is why they want you to join them, so that together you both can benefit and be around like-minded people. The focal point is on what they say, not necessarily how they dress, because they want you to be captivated with their offer. The Charmer often uses the following words and phrases during the ask:

- "It's the best thing that has ever happened."
- "Honestly, you do not want to miss out."
- "I know you feel the same way I do."
- "The time is now."

Advantages of the Charmer

The Charmer's style is inviting and fresh, which means that they are highly successful in grabbing your attention. If you had no idea who the Charmer was, after a few minutes with them, you would know exactly who they are and what they want. They are careful to select whom they wish to approach and engage because they have a keen eye on who really may be the next person to join them. They do not need a lot of time to get to the ask because their style is just to be direct. Long, lofty, and beat-around-the-bush conversations are not in their nature. The Charmer is totally comfortable in who they are, what they say, and how they dress. Even if someone does not care for them or finds them too direct, they smile, say, "Thank you," and go on to find someone who will join them in their pursuits.

Challenges for the Charmer

While the Charmer does take their time to carefully select the person they wish to win over, sometimes their direct approach is too direct. It may come off as too smug, too arrogant, or too assuming that the person they are engaging will naturally want to be a part of their professional or personal endeavors. The Charmer also has an internal clock. They will give the person a short amount of their time, and if it appears that the person is not leaning toward hearing more or asking questions that can lead to a promising agreement, the Charmer moves on.

Refinements for the Charmer

1. Try to spend some time with the people you meet, and get to know them by asking good open-ended questions before you talk about what you are promoting. If you do, you may be able to fashion your ask so that it will combine what they are interested in and what you need instead of sharing your needs before you know their interests.

2. Be careful that a strong tone of voice combined with a direct delivery does not sabotage your ask. If you have a direct style, make sure your tone of voice is not harsh, tough, or overbearing. Also, your direct style of asking may cause you to stand too close to the person you are asking, so be sure to maintain a healthy distance to give the person some room physically and mentally to consider your ask.

3. Give great consideration to the words you select when you ask. Instead of saying this: "My mission is to fix one hundred bicycles a year and to give them to anyone who needs one for transportation or pleasure. I'm looking for people like you who can contribute $250 this Christmas to give a child or an adult in need a new bike. Here's

my card," you can say this: "Over the past year, I discovered just how many children and adults don't have bikes for recreation or for essential transportation. Since bikes have been such a big part of my life, I started a nonprofit to give one hundred bikes, which cost $250 each, to children and adults in need each Christmas. Can I explain a bit more how you could get involved with our mission?"

This exercise of discovering the type (or types) of asker you are—and how you can make some refinements—will also be of great help when you think about how others around you personally and professionally make their ask. Pay attention to their characteristics, words, tone of voice, demeanor, body language, and style of dress. If you work with them, it may be easier now to understand how their asking style is a reflection of their personality or even their ability to do their job. For those you love—significant others, family, and friends—think about how they ask and how you can use your style with some refinements to be more in sync with each other's needs.

Next, we'll dive into all the preparation you need to make a great ask. At first you may think that it takes just a few steps, a few moments of consideration. I assure you that if you take the time to build the foundation to each ask, your success rate will increase exponentially. After all, you may have only one shot with one person when you make your ask. Let's make sure you are equipped and well prepared with the best preparation before you ask.

CHAPTER 3

The Three Rules of Asking—Be Prepared, Be Personal, and Be Present

She was a girl, maybe eight or nine years old at most. She sat in the front row and was quiet yet very attentive, with her father sitting next to her. He brought her to the event I was putting on for small businesses, nonprofits, and community groups in a suburb of Philadelphia. Whenever I am asked to come speak on a topic that is very important to a community, I always encourage the event planners to make sure that anyone who attends invites their family members as well. I've come to learn that the ask can have a much greater impact and more lasting power if as many people as possible in that area hear the same message at the same time, and that includes the family.

Usually people bring their spouses, partners, parents, family members, or business partners—but not their children. I worried at first whether this young girl would find what I was about to say useful or relevant in her life.

Throughout the session, this father-and-daughter team sitting directly in front me were "human sponges." They took in every word I had to say. I had just finished going over Laura's Five Laws of Asking, which you will read about in detail in the following chapters. Usually this brings out a lot of discussion because the simple steps behind each law really do work. At the end of the session, I always ask the audience if anyone has any questions or issues they'd like to work through. Our young girl's arm went up in a flash. It wasn't a gentle or slow raising of her arm; it was like a projectile aiming straight for the ceiling. I had a feeling she would jump up and blurt out her question if I didn't call on her first. Her stare of determination right at me made it impossible for me to look away. What she said still stuns me to this day: "Will these steps help me to stop being bullied?"

The room went dead silent. It was as if three hundred people stopped breathing. Some started looking at each other, some shaking their heads. Some were in disbelief at what they just heard. I glanced over to see her father. He never looked at her but kept staring at me. I had seconds to pull this all together because I honestly didn't know what to say or how to respond. If I asked her whether she could share some details about how she was being bullied and what these people were saying and doing to her, it might bring up all the terrible feelings she was experiencing. If I didn't ask her, then how would I know how to help her or even what to say? Before she said a word, her entire body language changed. She went from "I'm bursting to ask my question!" to "Gosh, I have to relive this pain." Her shoulders hunched down, and she stared at the floor. Her hands were clasped very tightly together in front of her. She looked lifeless, powerless, dejected, and rejected, as if whoever was doing this to her was right in front of her. She said only a few things about what happened. These bullies were her classmates, and they singled her out. They made fun of her, of how she dressed and how she talked, and it was always done around her friends, who just laughed. A double pain. They didn't do it to anyone else, just her. They made sure none of her teachers were around when they did it. It happened almost every day, and it wasn't stopping.

There are times in your life when you just want to dive in, give someone the biggest hug, and tell them it is all going to be fine. This was that moment for me, but I knew it wasn't the right thing to do in this situation. A hug would certainly feel good in the moment, but then what? Was it going to help her when she went home? I stopped this time and asked her, "What do you think could help you right now?" She straightened up a bit, unclasped her hands, and then—looking right at me—said, "Do you think if I ask them to stop, they will?" I looked around the room, and no one was moving. I honestly did not see this coming. Of all the questions I'd gotten up until then, this ranked way up there as one of the hardest to address.

"Honesty wins the day" is one of my favorite made-up mantras, and I needed it then. While I love to have the right answer with the right words and have the person who asked the question nod with a big smile, this was not going to be that moment. So I said to her, "I think if you ask, that would be great. But I also know we need to help you prepare for what they will say back. Then what you will say to them. You will need a strong voice, and you will need to stand as tall as you can and stare them down. Does that make sense?"

I could tell she was thinking this over. Her face scrunched up a bit, her eyebrows came down, her eyes got closer. Now everyone in the room was hanging onto her next words. She said, "I didn't think to ask them to stop, but now I know I have to. I want to. They are going to tease me, but I have to speak up and be ready. I know I have to at least try." I thought the room would explode with applause and bravas.

This young, honest, and brave girl just nailed it without me saying a word. My little "human sponge" got it, and it was her words, not mine, that told the audience the importance of preparing the ask. It had more impact on this audience than I could ever have made.

Later that day, I brought the father to the side of the room for a private conversation. I was very worried that I didn't fulfill his expectation (remember that is my major tempter from chapter 1). He said that he had come and had brought his daughter to see if there was something she could do first to put an end to this unwanted, aggressive behavior from kids who were supposed to be her friends. If not, he would have to get involved, but he really didn't want to unless it got out of hand. I gave him a lot of credit for empowering his daughter first before taking action. Then he said this "ask thing" had intrigued him, so he came to my session.

The daughter was across the room, smiling a bit and surrounded by adults. They all expressed empathy, kindness, and support. She looked lighter, happier, and more at ease. While I never heard from them after that day, and I will never know how things turned out, I do know our young girl, at a very early stage in her life, learned the power of preparation.

Know Your Audience

Now that you know how important it is to prepare your ask, we are going to explore some components of the preparation. When we talk about preparation, it is always about a series of questions we need to ask ourselves.

- How well do I really know the person I'm about to ask?
- Do I know what they are interested in right now?
- What can I ask them that may motivate them to help me reach my goal?
- What's in it for them?
- Will they help me because they want to or have to?
- How do I do this without jeopardizing any prior relationship I had with this person?

Yes, there is a lot more to this than just deciding whom you should ask and then giving it your best shot. Knowing at least some essential facts about the person you are about to ask is so important. This often comes up for people who need to raise money for a nonprofit, increase their customer or client base, or launch a new business where they don't know the people they are supposed to ask. The "cold call" you need to make is just that—cold—because you haven't found a connection to them before you reach out. Anyone can do some research on the internet on the people they wish to contact, which does provide great background information, but it is those personal and connective tidbits—those jewels, if you will—that will give you a greater chance of people at least hearing more about what you want.

Sean was all set to launch his own coaching business, having served as a paralegal for a national law firm for many years. He knew he wanted a different career path, so he took virtual executive coaching classes at an Ivy League university's advanced management program and was ready to open his business. He felt that his niche was coaching executives or anyone in a leadership and management role whose job it was to negotiate. His target clients were people in these roles who either felt that they did not have the personality for conflict, were never trained in conflict resolution, or despised negotiating but had to do it. He had his website, business cards, and logo. It wasn't investment money in his company that he was after. It was finding a steady stream of clients, paying clients, who would sustain his new business.

He told me he was too old and that he did not want to go to chamber of commerce or networking meetings to simply feel like a high school kid handing out résumés to get his first job washing dishes for a restaurant or parking cars. Now there's an image: a seasoned professional starting a new career yet feeling as if he were back in his teenage years! While he did "reach out" to a bunch of people who were "leads" from colleagues, nothing panned out. Each week, he was making several calls and sending emails to his leads, but those communications always stated what he had done in the past to get him to this point to be an executive coach and what he could offer that was unique from other coaches with less experience and fewer credentials. Sean did what many do when they reach out for the first time to people they do not know: sell and retreat. What is missing? Sean's interest in them. First and foremost, you need to be interested in the person you are contacting.

This actually is a lot easier than you think. The next time someone refers you or suggests that you contact that person, first tell the person who is giving you the contact that your relationship with them is what is most important to you. Tell them that anything they wish to share or not share is OK with you. It is a step most people miss, and then they get blindsided when that friend, colleague, relative, or neighbor suddenly acts a bit distant or seems to be less receptive to their outreach. Make sure you are totally in sync with the information they are about to share and how you will use it.

Next be ready with your questions of the person who is doing the referring. For Sean, the questions would have been the following:

- "Why do you think this person needs an executive coach?"
- "Is there any funny story I can share about you and this person to catch their interest?"
- "What hobbies or interests do they have?"
- "How do they like to be communicated with: telephone call, text, video chat, letter?"
- "What words should I use to perhaps pique their interest to learn more about what I do?"
- "How could I tell if they are speaking to me out of a favor to you or if they truly may want my services?"
- "Are there topics I should avoid?"
- "How do they like to be addressed?"

At first this may look like you are grilling or heavily interviewing your friend or colleague. My suggestion is that you pick and choose the questions you feel are most important and just naturally weave them into your conversation. This is exactly where you can get just one or two personal connectors that will grab the interest of the person you wish to ask. The last question ("How do they like to be addressed?") can speak volumes about the person and should not be overlooked. This is where assumptions really raise their ugly heads. If the person is a chief executive officer, a vice president, a major well-known and successful investor, an ambassador, or a president, there is an assumption that we have to act and speak more formally to them because they are in a position of authority. My suggestion is that you take a bit of time and find out whether this is what the person wants before you become more formal in your approach. You can get off to a really bad start either way if you don't get this right. The easiest and quickest way is to ask this the first time you connect or speak with them: "Would you prefer to be called *X*?" This way, they can let you know.

Mary was a major gifts officer for a very large and well-known conservation nonprofit. Her boss, Elliot, the CEO, had a personal friend, Chris, who was a billionaire, the president and CEO of one of the top real estate firms in the city. Elliot and Mary had talked about an idea they had to ask Chris to invest in a project with the conservation organization. The project was to renovate a major statue and the surrounding acreage that were right outside Chris's office and were part of the conservancy. The project plus the naming rights would cost $1 million. Both of them thought that this would be a good "starter gift" for Chris and that if he said yes and was pleased with the project, they, in time, could go back and ask him for a larger gift.

Elliot set up a meeting and told Mary it was best if she went alone because Elliot and Chris were such good friends that he would feel awkward. Mary was really nervous at first, but she had all her documents and a well-laid-out proposal. She had asked for gifts this large and larger before. When Mary arrived, Chris made her wait forty-five minutes past the meeting time. He called her in, never looking at her but instead at papers on his desk from his last meeting, and abruptly said, "Well, what do you want?"

Mary, now totally thrown off guard, said, "Chris, Elliot and everyone at the conservation organization have an idea in mind for you that we think you would be really interested in and would highlight all the great work your real estate firm has done for the city."

Before Mary could say another word, Chris said, "Young lady, who do you think you are speaking to? Never address me as 'Chris.'" Before Mary could apologize, he asked, "What's in your hand?"

Mary said it was a proposal they had crafted just for him.

He swiped it out of her hands, flipped through the page, saw the renderings and the price tag, and said, "This is ridiculous. My firm can do this project for $200,000." That was the end of the meeting, and Chris never made a gift to the conservation organization.

This story has so many red flags on what went wrong, but the part to focus on for now is that Chris was the type of individual who liked—well, demanded—to be addressed formally. It would have gotten the meeting off to a much better start. Perhaps then Mary would have had a window of opportunity to make her case that it is not the cost of construction that mattered but the fact that he would be recognized publicly to the whole city, that he and his firm would be known as one of the top and most generous donors to the conservation organization. That would have fed his ego nicely. The bottom line is this: before you make initial contact or go into any first-time meeting, know the person's title and how they would like to be addressed.

Select the Right Environment

How much time do you spend selecting just the right seat on an airplane, the right suite during your vacation, the right camping site for your trailer, the right decorations for a family or formal dinner, or the right venue to host a celebration? My guess is a lot of time because you want to set the right tone, the right atmosphere, for an important event or occasion. Atmosphere, tone, noise level, and comfort are so important for occasions we care about, and we wish to have only the best of times. This is so true when you start thinking

> The rule of selecting the right environment is to do your ask where the person you are asking is most comfortable.

about where to make your ask. The rule of selecting the right environment is to do your ask where the person you are asking is most comfortable. When selecting the right environment to make your ask, you have many choices:

- In person
- On the telephone
- In a text
- Over a live video chat, such as Zoom, Teams, or WebEx
- In an email
- In a written proposal or letter

Each of these choices of where to do your ask has pluses and minuses. Consider them in the following chart:

ENVIRONMENT	PLUSES	MINUSES
IN PERSON	You get to be with the person live, so you can look into their eyes and observe their body language. You have the advantage of not only listening to what the person has to say, but you can also observe their every move.	Depending on the setting, there can be outside distractions: waiters at a restaurant, interruptions at their office or yours, telephone calls at their home. You have to look your best, which takes time. You need high, positive energy and focus for the duration of your meeting.
ON THE TELEPHONE	It is convenient and easy to schedule. You do not have to get dressed up.	There are no visual cues for you to decipher whether the person is inclined to say yes. You may misinterpret their tone.
IN A TEXT	Your ask will be short and to the point. If the person you are asking likes to be direct, you will get your answer in a text or two.	You have to ensure that you have no misspellings and that you do not insert emojis or symbols that can turn off or offend the person. Tone is often difficult to determine in a text. For example, a person can be using humor when you may take their tone as serious.

IN A CLOUD-BASED VIDEO MEETING	You have a much better chance of getting the person sooner because there is no travel involved. It is second best to being live because you can see the person, read their body language, and quickly decipher their tone, as you can see them on the screen.	There may be distractions such as phone calls, family members or pets in the background, or outside noises like lawn mowers and garbage trucks. As with live meetings, you do need to look professional and presentable and remind yourself that in essence, you are really "in person." You will need to make sure your body language and tone of voice are positive with high energy.
IN AN EMAIL	You can quickly get to your ask and lay out all the terms, conditions, parameters, and benefits of your ask. It is quick and convenient to attach additional materials, videos, testimonials, and links to websites in an email.	People may open your email but never address it. When you do not hear back, you have to send reminder emails, which is time consuming. The subject line of your email may place it in their spam file, so you need to carefully select the right subject matter to catch their attention and motivate them to read the email.
IN A PROPOSAL OR LETTER	If you are a good writer, you may use your skills to be persuasive and convincing. It is easy to lay out all the facts, statistics, charts, and graphs for the person to read and decide at their convenience.	If you are not a good writer, it may take a lot of time for you to write it or hire someone to do your writing. There may be a tendency to include too much information, which may turn off the person or, worse, cause them to never read it. You have the burden of following up to make sure they received it, read it, and are ready to make a decision.

The first step is to find out which of the above would be the best atmosphere for the person you are about to ask. The easiest and fastest way to find that out is simply to ask: "Tracy, you and I have been speaking on the telephone in the past. I have this great opportunity that is right in line with your key interests that you shared with me. This is an important meeting, so would you prefer we meet in person, continue on the telephone, or perhaps set up a Zoom meeting?"

Don't fall into the trap that just because you have been communicating with the person on the telephone, the person wants to be asked on the telephone. People have their set ideas of exactly where they would like to make important decisions. Sometimes it just comes down to the person being bored or exhausted with talking on the telephone, so they would rather see you in person. Conversely, they may be überbusy with work or family matters, and a text or written communication is the best route for them at that time.

Once you know where the person wants to do the ask meeting, the second step is to make sure you have a stable and predictable environment. In his book *Atomic Habits*, James Clear talks about the importance environment has on your behavior: "If you want behaviors that are stable and predictable, you need an environment that is stable and predictable."[2] This is so true when you ask. You want an environment that is stable and predictable because that will place you in the right frame of mind when you make your ask. The fewer distractions that are present, the more focus the person will place on your ask. The chart below shows you how you can make each environment as stable and as predictable as possible:

IN PERSON	If at a restaurant, reserve a table in the far back corner, away from a bar area or kitchen.
	If outside, select a setting that is not around traffic or loud noises, and be aware of whether the person is sensitive to sunlight.
	At your office, be sure to put all telephones and cell phones on silent mode, and if possible put out things in your office that may be visual reminders of the benefits of your ask—for example, a real estate topography model for an investor or a photograph of children making their own ropes course for a camp.
	Let your staff and assistants know you are not to be disturbed.
ON THE TELEPHONE	If you are on a landline, turn off your cell phone.
	Always stand up because your voice is stronger, and you exude more energy.
	Do not look at your computer or phone.
	Let anyone in your home or office know you need *X* amount of time for quiet.
	If you are in your car, pull over, away from traffic, and find a quiet spot.
	If using your cell, ensure the reception is strong.

---

2   James Clear, *Atomic Habits* (New York: Avery, 2018).

IN A TEXT	Triple-check the spelling before you hit send.
	Be mindful of your tone. It is far too easy to be more casual in a text.
	Your ask is important, so do not use any abbreviated letters for words unless you know for sure that is how the person likes to communicate and has communicated with you in that way.
	There can be an assumption that once you send it, you will get a quick response. At the end of each text, let the person know the exact date you need your answer.
IN A CLOUD-BASED VIDEO MEETING	The rule here is to practice with the background before the meeting to make sure you look professional and presentable.
	Your background is your universe, so select wisely. Select the background that you think the person would enjoy seeing.
	Virtual backgrounds can make your head look distorted, so make sure you do not look like you are an avatar.
	Make sure your landline and cell phones are turned off.
	If you are doing it from home or your office, let people know you need X amount of time of quiet.
	Avoid doing an ask in a café or park or in your car because there may be others listening in; it can give the impression that your ask is not that important because you did not take the time to have a stable, private, secure, and professional environment.
	Always stand up because your voice is stronger, and you exude more energy.
	Remove anything around your computer, laptop, or cell phone that will distract you from focusing 100 percent on the person you are asking on the screen.
IN AN EMAIL	There are two rules. Rule 1: Make sure your subject line is compelling to open, not compelling to go immediately to the spam file.
	Rule 2: Keep it short. People will quickly see the body of an email, and if it is more than three short paragraphs,* they will leave it for another time or, worse, never get back to it.
	State what you want with the exact number and the exact date.
	Let them know you will call or text by X date to follow up.
	Check the spelling before you send.
IN A PROPOSAL OR LETTER	Proposals: Follow the proposal guidelines very carefully. Do not add additional material because you feel it will make it more persuasive.
	If you have been in steady contact with someone prior to this submission, make sure you reference those communications.
	Always ask them to acknowledge receipt of the proposal if you send it by email.
	Letters: This takes a bit of homework, so calculate as best you can from the time you mailed the letter to the time it was received. Give it three business days, and if you have not heard back, call them.
	Letters need to get to the point just as emails, using the model of three paragraphs with two sentences in each paragraph and no more.*

*For a hard copy sample of a three-paragraph email and three-paragraph letter,
go to www.ExpertonTheAsk.com.*

Have you ever said to yourself, "I'm doing far too many Zoom meetings, and I'm about to lose my mind?" Well, I have repeatedly, and I'm sure you have too. But there are some things that, oddly enough, I continue to like with cloud-based video meetings beyond the obvious that they are just so convenient. You can sit in a makeshift office or a real office; select a spot in a hotel, Airbnb, or Vrbo; and conduct business within the comfort and convenience of your setting.

I have a tip for you that will make you stand out in your Zoom or cloud-based video conferences. I referenced this above when we discussed how to create the best environment for your telephone calls and your video conferencing meetings. For telephone calls, even if you are contacting someone for the first time or making an ask, stand while you make your call. Whether you are the presenter or a participant in a video conferencing meeting or seminar, stand. This, of course, takes into consideration that you are physically able to stand and that it will not aggravate any existing injuries or cause you pain.

While you are on video, make sure your camera captures you standing, not sitting, so you may have to prop your computer or cell phone up a bit. When you stand, you have stronger body language and a stronger voice, and you bring a stronger sense of energy. Even if you are sitting upright in a chair and have the perfect office or home setting, your voice is not as strong. There is too much temptation during the call or the video session to look at whatever is around you, and then you give the impression that you are simply less present. A stronger voice and the visual presence of your body language show people you are engaged and in the moment, and everyone can feel you have brought a stronger sense of energy to the meeting.

I stand mainly because I can concentrate better, breathe better, and speak better. When I stand up, my voice has a much better projection, and I just feel more alive and engaged. Try it a few times and see if you see and feel the difference in how you feel and how others look at and respond to you.

Your Tone Is Your Superpower

Since I now have you standing, what tone of voice are you using when you are making these important calls and video meetings? Most people overlook this and fail to see how it really can make or break any conversation you may have leading up to or at your ask. I learned this a while ago when a group gave me an audio link to a session we had just done for a women's networking group. I listened in horror. I must have used the word "absolutely" a thousand times when I was asked a question. If that was not bad enough, it was the way that I said it that must have turned everyone off. It sounded trite after a while, too repetitive. I didn't like it because I came off cocky, like a know-it-all. It was a real eye-opener for me.

Psychology professor Albert Mehrabian at the University of California, Los Angeles, laid out the concept called the 7-38-55 rule in his book *Silent Messages*. The concept divided into percentages how we communicate emotions:[3]

- 7 percent spoken words
- 38 percent tone of voice
- 55 percent body language

Since the ask is an "emotional firecracker" with emotions running quite high, it is important to drill down and see how important your

---

3   Albert Mehrabian, *Silent Messages* (California: Wadsworth, 1971).

tone of voice is when you ask. While the selection of your words when you make your ask is incredibly important, as you will see in the later chapters, my expression is "Your tone is as important as your words." Tone has been called the foundation of customer service,[4] the basis of whether you make a sale or not.[5] Tone also gauges whether you and your company will be successful with customer acquisition, particularly in social media and B2B business. It can drive customer demand and increase the products people buy.[6]

The best way to test out your tone when you are meeting in person, on a call, or video conference is supereasy. Script a short conversation you need to have with someone, and use your phone to record it. Record your short rehearsal conversation, and play it back over and over again. Do you like the tone you are using? Are you speaking in any of the following ways?

- Speaking too loudly?
- Speaking in a harsh tone?
- Speaking too softly?
- Speaking too apologetically?
- Speaking with too much or too little energy?
- Speaking in a condescending manner?
- Speaking too stiffly—too "corporate"?
- Speaking in a tone that is too laid back?
- Using the same words?
- Using "um" too much?

---

4   Paldesk, "The Importance of Tone of Voice in Customer Service," Paldesk, accessed February 15, 2023, https://www.paldesk.com/the-importance-of-tone-of-voice-in-customer-service/.

5   Nick Bondaugh-Winn, "Why Tonality Matters in Sales and How to Improve it," December 2021, accessed February 15, 2023, https://www.hbwleads.com/blog/why-tonality-in-sales-matters-and-how-to-improve-it/.

6   Renato Hübner Barcelos, Danilo C. Dantas, and Sylvian Sénécal, "Watch Your Tone on Social Media," Baylor University Keller Center for Research, accessed February 15, 2023, https://www.baylor.edu/business/kellercenter/news.php?action=story&story=209670.

Keep recording your voice and making refinements. Trust me, it takes time. If you are like me and use one word subconsciously over and over, you may want to ask a colleague, audience member, or friend to let you know if you used it too much. What we hear is often not what we think we said.

My second tip is to have a mirror in front of your computer screen, in your home or office where you typically make calls and take your video meetings. When you speak, look directly into the mirror. I did, and again what a surprise. I had a wicked head tilt to the right. Try tilting your head one way, and see how it alters how you speak, what you say, and the tone you use. It won't be pretty. The mirror will correct any misalignment you make when speaking with a person live, via phone, or on video.

> What we hear is often not what we think we said.

If you think that this is so basic and you have this all in check, remember this story. A high-ranking university officer—we shall call him Marcelo—who knew quite well that a wealthy and very generous university donor, Irina, had set up a time for the two of them to consider Irina's next gift. Irina was the president of a major book publishing company and had made several six-figure gifts to the university's business school. Marcelo had prepared and scripted exactly what he would say to her, with an excellent, well-laid-out proposal. He would ask her to name the university's new Women's Entrepreneurial Communications program at the university, and the cost to name it was $5 million.

Irina agreed it would be best to have the meeting at her apartment because she worked late hours, and this was the only time and the only space where she felt they could have their important quiet, undisturbed time together. Marcelo arrived at her home, and things were going very well. They each talked about their recent vacations.

Marcelo smoothly transitioned the conversation to thanking Irina for the exemplary gifts she had given to the university and then let her know that he had an opportunity that he and others at the university thought would be something of great interest to her. He laid out the parameters of the proposal, what it would mean to have her as the founder and mentor for the program, and stated that it would be a $5 million investment for this naming opportunity. He even told her he had other donors he thought would contribute to sustaining the new program if she were the one to first make this opportunity happen.

Irina turned to him and said, "What? Are you kidding me?"

Marcel was stunned and thought immediately she was outraged by the proposed amount to fund the program. Before he could even speak, she said, "While I might have been interested in considering it and hearing more, the way you just said it sounded like you expected me to do it." And just like that, the $5 million gift proposal fizzled away. She never gave to the university again.

Your tone can and will make or break your ask. Take the time within the next few days to record your voice and ask a colleague, friend, or family member for some honest feedback about how you come across when you're asking for something that is important to you. Remember, your tone is your superpower. It can invite people to hear more and say yes to your ask, or it can turn them off, and your ask will fizzle away.

Are You Listening—Really Listening?

Anna was miserable at work. Her boss, the CEO she rarely could meet with, decided that he had too much responsibility and hired a personal friend as the organization's chief operating officer (COO). This meant that Anna reported to him, not the CEO. When I met with Anna, she was totally distraught. She was asked to put together a major presentation in front of the entire board, justifying why they had raised less money with more staff. Anna felt that the CEO and now the COO would use this moment to fire her. In the past, they had questioned why she had expanded her staff and why she was not bringing in her revenue projections, and they had pointed out how other peer organizations were far exceeding their revenue streams and expanding their markets. Anna showed me her PowerPoint presentation, and while it was good, it said all over it, "I'm a good person; I'm doing the job, and you just can't see it."

Drawing upon my days as a litigation attorney, I told Anna that cases and confrontational situations are "won on facts": "Stick to the facts. Lay out the facts with suggested solutions in plain and simple terms and in a calm voice, which would win over some board members and, in time, your CEO and COO." I told her that she had to eliminate anything in the presentation that screamed, "I'm doing the right thing," and instead neutrally lay out the statistics, benchmarks, as well as the challenges the organization had had in the past with suggested solutions. For two hours, we went over this, and all Anna could say was, "But it's in there," "I've tried this before," and "I've explained why we are where we are today, and it's the board's lack of involvement over the past few years."

Defensive, defensive, defensive. And you can imagine the tone of voice she had throughout our meeting: sharp, dismissive, and filled with anger that she was not being recognized for her talent and expertise. Our meeting ended, and I walked Anna to the spot where her Uber was picking her up. I told her to go home and think about how she could calmly make this presentation and use a little humor to lighten her up and set an easy tone for the meeting. I shared with her that whenever someone in an authoritative position questions you in a large setting—in this case, her CEO, COO, and presumably some of her board members—where you feel you are being judged, and you need an immediate answer, don't answer. Instead, show a genuine smile with an air of appreciation and say, "Gee, let me think about this."

She automatically said: "I always use humor. I'm just not showing that now."

"Exhibit A," I said. "You are not listening to what I said. You are trying to justify why you are right and they are wrong. You're justifying why you have done everything, they haven't seen your progress, they have done nothing to help your work, and they have not listened to you. But the fact is you're not listening to me now, and I'm not sure you are really preparing yourself to listen to them."

"To listen well is to figure out what's on someone's mind and demonstrate that you care enough to want to know," states Kate Murphy in *You're Not Listening: What You're Missing & Why It Matters.*[7] This book was recommended to me by my good friend and client Shelly Power, executive director of the Philadelphia Ballet. Shelly and Kate are very good friends, and Shelly thought this would be a good book for me to read. It remains one of my favorites. Even on the inside cover, Kate is speaking my language: "Listening is about curiosity and patience—about asking the right questions in the right way."

You simply cannot begin to even think of asking for anything and expect really great results unless you have practiced the art of active listening. I have to say in the past I was a horrible listener, really terrible. I would just dig deeply into my work, convince myself that I was so prepared with all the "what ifs" that may come up that I never factored in the pause, the discipline, the straight look into someone's eyes with the body language that says, "I'm present. I'm listening to

---

7   Kate Murphy, *You're Not Listening: What You're Missing & Why It Matters* (London: Harvill Seeker, 2020).

you." I learned this the hard way. My boss at the attorney general's office in Philadelphia, John Shellenberger, came to one of my trials. I was all of twenty-nine years old. It was a First Amendment case, the area of law I love, but it was not going well. The attorney assigned to the case who had been working on it for nine months took ill, and the day before the trial started, I got assigned to the case and knew absolutely nothing about it. I would have to read all the depositions, go over the witness list, meet my witnesses in court for the first time, and find out what discussions had taken place with the judge and who my opposing counsel were. I cried the whole way home on the SEPTA bus, thinking I was sunk.

The case involved a well-known activist who claimed the state police violated his First Amendment rights when his followers, the picketers, were told by the state police to move back because they were on private property. He claimed that some of the police used the picket signs to move them to public property. Whenever someone sued the state office or state officers in a civil action, the attorney general's office represented them. I stayed up the whole night studying First Amendment law, but it was of no use. The activist was represented by a huge law firm with three male lawyers, and there was me, at five-foot, two-inches tall, representing the Commonwealth of Pennsylvania.

John came in and was observing the trial. At the noon break, he came up to me and said, "Did you hear it?" I was thinking, *Hear what? I thought I heard everything.* John told me that on direct examination, the activist said he was standing at the spot with his back to the state police. John said there was no way the activist could have seen what the police were doing. Light bulb. I never heard it. On cross-examination, I asked this activist, "You were standing here, facing this way, correct?" He said yes. Needless to say, we won the case. From that moment on, I won many more cases on cross-examination because I learned to listen—really listen.

Listening takes constant practice, and later on, when I transitioned from law to fundraising, my listening skills slipped. I was fundraising for an incredible hospital that treats people with heart and lung diseases, regardless of their ability to pay. What an amazing mission, and I loved this job. One of the donors I was working with was Barbara, who lived in a very wealthy area of New Jersey. While I did ask to meet her personally, she always declined my invitation. Instead, she was happy to have brief telephone conversations from time to time. Barbara's husband was a former patient at the hospital, having had heart surgery. While he did live for many years post his surgery, he died a few years later from other health complications. Barbara had given the hospital a few charitable gifts over the years, and I, being the persistent one, always asked if she would be open to meeting with me so I could thank her personally. She finally said yes and specifically said, "Wear something comfortable like sneakers or boots. I want to show you my garden."

Did I listen? Yes, but I thought she was potentially going to be a major donor to the hospital, so I should show up looking a bit more businesslike. I wore a button-down shirt, dress pants, and flat shoes, but they were not sneakers or boots. When I arrived, she opened the door and said to me, "I guess you didn't listen to what I said when I invited you. It's important you see my garden and understand that this gets me through the grief of losing my husband."

I wanted to sink into the ground. I apologized, explained why I dressed the way to make myself more presentable, and then said to her, "I heard you, and this is on me. You've taught me an invaluable lesson. Can we set a new time for me to come, and I promise I will be dressed to spend our time in your garden?" She said yes, and we met a few months later. I wore my khaki pants, a polo shirt, and boots. Her "garden" was on two hundred acres, and it included an additional two hundred acres of horse farms. You are probably thinking that I should have done my research and known that she lived on so much land. Mind you, this was back in the day when prospect research was getting to know the person in person, and we did not have the amazing search engine tools to find out these details that we have today. When I left, she had an envelope on the table next to the door with my name on it. She picked it up and said, "This is for the hospital." I asked her if I should open it now or when I returned to the office. Barbara, being Barbara, said, "That's your choice." I thanked her, got into my car, and drove three blocks away. Of course, I lashed into the envelope, opening it, and there was a check of $25,000 with a note thanking me for coming and for being part of her life. She said that this gift would be the first of many large gifts she would be making to the hospital. I learned to listen that day, to really listen, and the important lesson for me was to listen with presence.

To listen with presence means there is nothing else in the world going on but the person in front of you and what they have to say. When you ask, you need to listen to the person's every word and be present, and show you are present, and then and only then can you make the right response to their ask. In the next chapter, you will see how important listening with presence is, especially when someone responds to your ask. It's a simple formula that I call the 75/25 Rule. You talk 25 percent of the time; they talk 75 percent of the time. We will really see this rule in action when we get to the next chapter.

This leads us right into Laura's Five Laws of Asking. Listening with presence is a thread that runs throughout these five laws. Now that you have all the preparation skills, you are ready to go through these five laws that will not only change the way you ask but also change the way you think and change the way you show up at each ask. They will make your life so much easier because you can use these tools over and over again. They are timeless, they apply to anyone of any age living anywhere—and best of all, they work!

Takeaways

- Every ask requires careful preparation.
- Before you make your ask, ask yourself how well you know the person. Take the time to find out some important details about them so that the focus of your ask is about them, not you.
- You have many choices in the way you can make your ask, and each has pluses and minuses: in person, on the telephone, in a text, over a live video, or in a proposal or letter. Select the one that makes the person you are asking the most comfortable.
- If you want your ask to be stable and predictable, you need to select a stable and predictable environment.
- Your tone is your superpower. Record a conversation and play it back. Is this the tone you want for your ask?
- Listening with presence will ensure that you will have laser focus on your ask.

CHAPTER 4

Laura's Five Laws of Asking—Law 1

Know Exactly What You Want with Numbers and Dates

Paul was the kind of guy who made you just want to sit down and listen to his stories forever. He always had a huge smile, even when he was sharing the most horrific and death-defying work situations. There was the time when he was being flown in a helicopter, lowered down on a rope, with gale force winds at forty knots per hour, so that he could land on this island and search for improvised explosive devices. Laughing, as if this were just a drill or he were an actor in *The Matrix*, he said, "Nah, there was nothing there." Or the time when he was in charge of finding one of the biggest drug cartels in South America. Before he left for the trip, Paul would say, "Don't look for me on Facebook for a while, and if my mother starts asking for me, tell her I'm traveling for a week down south. But don't tell her how far south."

Paul had a successful career in the military and in the Federal Bureau of Investigation and then specialized in international security.

He would travel from Russia to South America, to small, remote areas in the United States, never sharing the exact details of his travel and not bothering to mention that his life could be in danger. At six feet two and two hundred pounds of solid muscle, he was someone you really did not want to mess with. At the same time, he had this boyish, soft quality with an intoxicating smile that made you just want to hug him. Yet with his all his superhero adventures, from combating drug lords and conducting surprise raids to securing public arenas, Paul had what he called a weak spot. He simply could not ask for money for himself, especially when it came time to negotiate a salary for a new position.

Here is this tower of power, a sought-after defender of our safety, but when it comes to getting the money he is worth, he can't get the words out. He feels that being paid slightly more than his previous job is fine with him and that no one would be crazy enough to pay him more.

> Organization, structure, and focus are my three go-to remedies that we all need to get out of our own heads and to plow forward on a pressing need or a challenge.

Then a major, high-paying opportunity came his way. This company had the assets to hire Paul at a rate of twice as much as he was currently making. While Paul realized this was a fantastic new job and that the company could pay him well, he knew that they would ask him first what his salary requirements were.

The flood of doubts came rushing in as to what he should ask for in terms of his salary. Here were some of his concerns, which may sound familiar to you:

- Should I ask them for just a little more than I was already making?
- What if they ask me what I was making in my last job?

- People tell me to ask for a higher six-figure salary, but I'm not worth that.
- They said they'd give me a bonus, too, so I don't really need to go that high on salary.
- I'm just doing the same job I did before. Why should I ask for a higher salary?

Organization, Stucture, Focus

If you "listen" to all his concerns, Paul was talking himself out of asking for a higher salary before he even had the conversation with his prospective employer. Take a deeper dive into his concerns, and what do you hear? He doesn't feel that he deserves more money and that he has probably struggled with money for a while. Anytime anyone has one of these circular conversations in their head, especially when it involves money and self-worth, it is the time to bring in my three favorite remedies: apply organization, structure, and focus.

ORGANIZATION	You need to organize your thoughts to optimize your success.
STRUCTURE	Structure secures your stability and strength to make your best choices.
FOCUS	Where focus goes, success grows.

Organization, structure, and focus are my three go-to remedies that we all need to get out of our own heads and to plow forward on a pressing need or a challenge. They are the backbone—the foundation, if you will—needed before you can apply my Five Laws of Asking.

Using Paul as an example, I demonstrate here how organization, structure, and focus can help anyone muscle thorough questionable thoughts and ideas about getting paid what they are worth prior to asking for the amount:

ORGANIZATION	You need to organize your thoughts to optimize your success.	I worked hard in my career. I deserve this new job at a much higher pay than my previous job. They said that they value my experience, so they will be expecting me to want to be paid well. I have to stop thinking that this is just moving up within an existing job that has set pay rates.
STRUCTURE	Structure secures your stability and strength to make your best choices.	They contacted me. I'm in the driver's seat. Let me do some research as well as calling around to get a good take on what the market is paying for my level of experience. I have my current job, so I'm stable, and nothing is at risk.
FOCUS	Where focus goes, success grows.	Let me research this company to make sure I want them as much as they want me. Once I decide I want it, I'll give it 100 percent of my attention.

Now that we have the foundation of organization, structure, and focus, it is time for Laura's Five Laws of Asking. I have some guidelines about applying these laws that I have tested over many years:

- They need to be done in order. No skipping around.
- As you will see in Law 2, when I say, "Write," I mean to write it down the old-fashioned way with pen to paper, to type it on your computer, or to make a note on your cell.
- They take practice and patience. Repeat the laws, and take notes where you think you could do better. I have my running list of where I can improve.
- Do not "reserve" these laws for your mega-asks. Use them for any size ask.
- Reward yourself, regardless of the response you get. Remember, the win is not the result but that you made the ask. When you

come off the intense focus of wanting to hear "yes," watch the "yes" come to you.

- It's time to dive in.

Laura's Five Laws of Asking

Law 1: Know exactly what you want, with numbers and dates.

Law 2: Write down fifteen things you think the person will say, and then write down your response to each one.

Law 3: Deliver with confidence; it's time to shine.

Law 4: Reiterate what you think you heard.

Law 5: Plan your next move at the end of your ask.

Law 1: Know Exactly What You Want, with Numbers and Dates

This sounds so simple, yet it is the first place that people mess up. When you hear

- "I need a raise,"
- "I need a promotion,"
- "I need more money for my new entrepreneurial project,"
- "I need more people to join,"
- "I need a vacation,"
- "I need more time with my boyfriend,"
- "I need my children to do more around the house,"
- "I need more clients,"
- "I need more sales,"
- "I need more gratitude," or

- "I need to be heard,"

what is missing? These are wishes; they are not asks. Successful asks have these two main components: specific numbers and specific dates. Without these specifics, you are telling the world what you need, but no one knows at what quantity or what time you want them. That leaves your asks in a dead zone because you have no call to action. Look at the difference between what you need, what is not an ask, and what is an ask:

WHAT YOU NEED	NOT AN ASK	AN ASK
A raise	"I want a raise because I've done so much extra work."	"I would like a $10,000 raise by December 1 of this year; let me explain why."
A promotion	"I wanted to be promoted to the open position."	"I would like to be promoted to the open position of vice president by June 1 of this year."
More money for a start-up	"I need to launch my new business, and I'm looking for an investor."	"In order to successfully launch my new business, I need an initial investment of $250,000 by March 31 of this year."
More members	"I'm in charge of the conference, and I need more people to sign up."	"The conference is November 15. I need one hundred additional people to sign up by November 1 for this to be profitable."
A vacation	"I'm exhausted. I need the time off to take a vacation."	"I have two weeks left on my vacation time. I'm requesting to take off starting August 22, returning to the office on September 5."
Your significant other to spend more time with you	"Don't you agree that we need more 'us' time?"	"I know our work has been interfering with our time. How about we agree that by Wednesday each week, we come up with a plan of how we can spend either all day Saturday or Sunday with each other?"
Your children to do more	"You three need to clean your rooms; this place is a mess."	"You three, each morning before you come downstairs, you need to make your beds. By Friday at 5:00 p.m. each week, I need you to clean your rooms, which means clothes are off the floor and in the hamper, and books, toys, and games are put away."
More clients	"In order to take my business to the next level, I need more clients."	"Each quarter of the calendar year, I am going to get ten new clients."
More sales	"Our team revenue numbers are low; midyear, we need to ask our existing customers for additional business."	"Team, in order to end the year strong, I need each of you to bring in an additional 20 percent over your projected goal by December 31 of this year."

To have more gratitude	"I really do need to take the time away from everything and become more grateful for the things I have in my life."	"I'm truly blessed, and I so appreciate all the good things that continue to come to me and those I love. Each morning before my feet touch the floor, I will take three minutes and list all the things I am grateful for."
To be heard	"I feel like every time I speak up in class, no one listens or understands what I am talking about."	"I am about to share my top two ideas on this topic. I would appreciate it if you would let me know what you think about my two ideas right after I speak. Your feedback is invaluable."

Do you see and hear the difference between asking when you do not add specific amounts and specific times? You fall back into the arms of our three tempters, luck, chance, and time. Hoping for luck that you will get it, even though what you asked for is so vague. Taking a chance that someone will fill in the blank for you and know the quantity that you want and the date you want it. And I don't believe the adage that "time heals all" in any ask. Time is never on your side when you don't say the exact time that you want something to happen.

> Successful asks have these two main components: specific numbers and specific dates. Without these specifics, you are telling the world what you need, but no one knows at what quantity or what time you want them.

CHAPTER 5

Laura's Five Laws of Asking—Law 2

*Write Down Fifteen Things You Think
the Person Will Say—and Then Write
Down Your Response to Each One*

Have you ever been in a situation in which you have an important ask to make, and you just know that a boss, coworker, customer, donor, friend, or family member is going to pelt you with questions, and it may make you look like you don't know what you're talking about? We have all been there. You probably start going over in your head what they will say and what you will say, and before you know it, you have a colossal headache. What is worse, you do come across unprepared and unknowledgeable because it is very difficult to recall, on the spot, the responses that sounded so wonderful when you were thinking about them.

This can all be easily resolved by a simple two-step action. First, you need to write down fifteen things you think the person will say to your ask. Second, you need to write fifteen things you will say to each of the fifteen responses you think you will receive. If you think this takes time, it sure does. Is it worth it? You bet.

Stephanie had a big problem on her hands. She was responsible for a major live two-day conference that was coming up in three months. Her attendance was low. In addition to not making her attendance goal, low attendance meant unsatisfied vendors for lack of foot traffic. That meant the vendors would be hard to secure for next year's conference. Stephanie was in my training session for Kellen, one of the world's largest providers of management and services to associations and trade organizations. We were going through the Five Laws of Asking, and she volunteered to use her challenge as a case study.

I asked her, "What is it you want?"

She said, "More members for my conference." Can you hear the buzzer violation going off for Law 1? She then corrected herself and said, "I need 115 more members."

We were getting close, but we were not on home plate. I asked, "By when?"

Then she got it. "I need 115 more members by October 14." One law down, four to go.

Now this is the fun part. I asked her to give me fifteen responses she would get when she asked someone to join her conference. With some help from her colleagues at the training, she came up with these fifteen responses, which I asked her to write down:

1. "Who are your speakers?"
2. "Can I pay for just one day?"
3. "What makes this year's conference different from last year's?"
4. "Your conference location is too far from where I live."
5. "I don't have the money, and work will not pay for my conference."
6. "I don't have the time to devote to a two-day conference."

7. "I checked the flights, and they are expensive and not good times for me."
8. "What other members are going?"
9. "What celebrities will be there, and will I have access to them?"
10. "What new vendors are coming?"
11. "Will the vendors give my company a discount if I attend the conference?"
12. "My boss won't let me attend."
13. "We have used our conference money from our budget."
14. "If I bring five people from my company, will we get a group discount?"
15. "Tell me three things specific to my industry that I will learn at this conference."

At first, it is hard to produce fifteen responses. Usually people get to five or six responses, and then they hit a wall. What else could a person say to your ask? As you see above, it just takes a little thought to recall responses you probably have heard before. So take a few minutes now, and think about an ask you need to do in the coming weeks or next month. Write down fifteen things you think the person will say. If you get stuck, hearken back to previous conversations you have had with the person you want to ask. Think of other asks you made and what people said as responses to you.

The beauty of this exercise is that once you have your fifteen, you just keep adding to the list. I'll never forget one time I was asking for an initial investment of $2 million for a campaign from a person I knew very well. He looked me squarely in the eyes, leaned forward, and said to me, "Laura, what makes you think I have $2 million?" Well, that went on the list. You see, while you will have your tailored fifteen responses to each ask you make, when you hear something that you did not expect, just add it to the list. Every time I share that story, people are always asking me, "What did you say to him?"

Simple. I said, "I have no idea if you have $2 million [because really, at any moment in time, no one can truly know if the person has those assets], but what I do know is that our leaders are counting on you to do this."

He just smiled, sat back, and said, "OK, I'm in." I sweated that entire meeting, but I learned an invaluable lesson: always be adding to your response list.

We have down the first step to Law 2: write down fifteen things you think the person will say to your ask. It is time we do the second step in Law 2: write down what you will say to each response. Keeping with the example of Stephanie and her need to get 115 additional members by October 14, I list here some sample ways to respond:

1. **"Who are your speakers?"**
   We have lined up two keynote speakers [name who they are]; we have the top three of the most sought-after speakers who rarely agree to speak at conferences.

2. **"Can I pay for just one day?"**
   Yes, of course we have a daily rate. Can I guide you into selecting the day that would benefit you the most?

3. **"What makes this year's conference different from last year's?"**
   We love that question. Based on our surveys from last year, we have factored in more downtime and meeting spaces for networking.

4. **"Your conference location is too far from where I live."**

I am so sorry to hear this. Might you have any business in this area that you could do before or after the conference?

5. **"I don't have the money, and work will not pay for my conference."**
    That is troubling to hear. We wish all employers saw the benefit of excellent outside educational opportunities for their employees. Please consider putting in now a budget item for you to attend next year. Also check back with your employer between now and the conference. Sometimes budget line items get shifted, and there may be funds for you to attend.

    > I learned an invaluable lesson: always be adding to your response list.

6. **"I don't have the time to devote to a two-day conference."**
    That is unfortunate and understandable. We will be offering a taped version of the entire conference at a reduced fee from the conference. Can I sign you up for this great benefit?

7. **"I checked the flights, and they are expensive."**
    Airlines can be harsh on business travelers this time of year. Just a suggestion, but try from time to time between now and the conference. If the plane is not full, they may lower the price, which will make it possible for you to attend.

8. **"What other members are going?"**

   We have an app for the conference that all registered members can access, so once you register, you will have full access. Is there any particular member or area of members you're interested in?

9. **"What celebrities will be there, and will I have access to them?"**

   For our VIP membership level, you will be seated in the front rows and have the opportunity to have your picture taken with [name the person or persons].

10. **"What new vendors are coming?"**

    We are thrilled to announce that [name the vendor or vendors] has/have agreed to attend. We have been asking them to join our conference for two years. They see the value proposition and want to meet great members like you.

11. **"Will the vendors give my company a discount if I attend the conference?"**

    While we do not have control over what the vendor discount will be, we assure you that you will have the time to spend with them so that you can ask them that question directly.

12. **"My boss won't let me attend."**

    That is unfortunate. Would it be helpful if I spoke to your boss or sent some information or testimonials from our prior attendees?

13. **"I'm not sure this conference will help me advance in my job."**

    Why don't you share a bit about what you do, and then I can go through the sessions with you to see how they can help you in ways you might not have thought of?

14. **"If I bring five people from my company, would we get a group discount?"**

    Five would be fantastic. Yes, we are open to that discussion.

15. **"Tell me three things specific to my industry that I will learn at the conference."**

Here is your chance to synthesize the top three learnings and make them as practical and industry tailored as possible.

This is a good base for you to adapt to what you need to be successful in Law 2. Remember, it has two parts. Once you start your fifteen responses, I know you'll be up to twenty-five, then fifty, and then continually adding more to your list. Your response to each does not have to be original each time. I like to say that you can "repurpose" some answers to people's responses. That is totally fine. Just be sure you are specifically addressing each response.

CHAPTER 6

Laura's Five Laws of Asking—Law 3

Deliver with Confidence; It's Time to Shine

You may only have one opportunity to make your ask, so you have to bring on your A game. This means you have to be focused with energy and filled with positivity. A person can "see" right through you, even if you are on the phone and not in person. Think for a minute when you had someone on the line, and you could tell they were distracted, multitasking, or speaking or whispering to someone else. How did you feel? Not great because this person was not devoting their time or attention on you.

Here are some special tips to help you have confidence for each ask:

1. **Stand up.**

   Yes. As we've already discussed, it is important that you stand when you are on Zoom or on a call. Naturally when you are in person doing your ask over coffee or in the person's home or office, you would be sitting down. When you are not in person, stand up. Your voice projects better, and you sound like you have energy and enthusiasm. Many asks receive yes answers just because the person sounded solid and confident.

Have you ever gone to a wine store that was having a tasting? If the person doing the tasting is sitting down behind the table with the open wine bottles and glasses, looking down at a cell phone, would this motivate you to go over and ask to sample the wine? What if the person is standing, waiting to greet you and ask if you would you like to sample some wine? The simple act of standing up gives a signal that the person wants to engage with you. There is more energy, and chances are that you would be more apt to sample some of the promoted wines. When you make any ask where you are not doing it in person, stand up. Your ask will feel more alive, and you will be more present.

> Many asks receive yes answers just because the person sounded solid and confident.

2. **Your eyes should be focused.**

It is easy to look down, particularly if you are nervous. The tendency can be to avoid eye contact, thinking that you will forget what you want to say if you look the person in the eyes. The problem is that if you don't, the person is going to think you are not sincere, not totally into what you are asking for, and they will likely give you a courteous "I have to think about it" response. You want a *yes* response, so let's get you there. Practice with friends or family, speaking to them without looking at anything else but them. Take a small subject, such as when they ask you how your day went or what plans you have for the weekend. Have the entire conversation just looking at them, and feel how present you are and how they appreciate your undivided attention.

3. **Hang a mirror.**

A while ago when I was making many cold calls and networking calls on my phone, I was so wrapped up in getting the right words out that I never did a body check to see what positions my head or body were in. Anytime you make a call (and now of course you will be standing up), make sure you look at the mirror and align your head, neck, and shoulders so that they are straight. First of all, it is great for your posture. Second, when your body is aligned, you simply have a feeling of more power and more control, and you have a positive presence.

Zoom and other video conferencing platforms have made it easy for us to see what we look like to others when we fit into the tiny square on the screen. I would still recommend that you have a mirror behind your computer so that you can get a better picture of yourself before you hop on that Zoom call.

CHAPTER 7

Laura's Five Laws of Asking—Law 4

Clarify What You Think You Heard

I was all geared up to make the biggest ask for money I had ever made in my lifetime: $15 million. I practiced, I rehearsed, I changed outfits seven times, and I put on my lucky jewelry. The man I was asking knew me, and he was a very active member of the organization that would be the beneficiary of what would become the largest gift to this group. I had my written list of over thirty responses; I thought about what he would say and what I would say back. With a deep breath and laser-focused eyes, I asked him for $15 million, and it went like this:

"As chair and the leader of this campaign, you know that your gift will not only be transformational, but it will also give us the lift to attract similar impactful gifts. We ask you now to consider making a $15 million gift, which will be the largest gift to date for this organization. Can we count on you to do this?"

Then the room was filled with excruciating silence. It felt like a year went by, but in reality, it was only a matter of seconds. He looked me straight in the eye and said, "I have to think about it."

I had of course prepared my response and said, "Of course. Take the time you need. We are grateful that you are considering a gift of this magnitude."

His response stunned me and formed the basis of Law 4. He replied, "I didn't say I needed more time. I want to think about how I can do this, part stock, part via my will."

Now what just happened here? What mistake did I make? I assumed (yes, we are back to one of our two tempters) that when he said he had to think about it, he needed more time. In the statement "I have to think about it," do you see the word *time*? No. That was an assumption on my part. The law here is that you have to be on the same page as the person you are asking. Your only job is to find out what the "it" is. I have to think about "it"—what is the "it?" The way

> **The law here is that you have to be on the same page as the person you are asking.**

you find out (surprise, surprise) is to ask. Here is the way I suggest you do it, and it has served me well ever since. When you hear "I have to think about it," say:

"Thank you, [insert their name or title]. To the extent you feel comfortable, can you share with me what you are thinking about? I am here to help you."

Then remain silent. This response is so important for you to make for several reasons. First, it puts both of you on the same page. People will share with you what their "it" is, and now you will know. Otherwise, you will be trying to get a definitive answer, thinking it's one thing, while the person you just asked is going in another thought direction. Second, I just love using this technique because it brings the person closer to you. When you say, "I'm here to help you," you are bringing the person in, letting them know you can work it out together, rather than leaving it up to them to do all the work deciding. I like to think of it as a verbal hug. You are bringing them closer, not leaving them high and dry to figure this out on their own. Third, if you do not fully understand what the person needs to think about, you probably will say something like I did or other common responses, such as one of these:

- "Terrific. I'll get back to you next week."
- "What more information do you need?"
- "Whom else do you need to talk to while making this important decision?"
- "Is the amount too high?"
- "Are there other groups asking you for a similar large gift?"

Just read all the assumptions in all of these responses. What makes this worse is that if you make all these assumptions, you have pushed back the timeline to get a definitive response. How can you possibly contact this person at a later time when you don't know what they are thinking about? What's left for you to say? You wind up saying some trite thing, like "Have you had the chance to think about it?"

> My rule for whatever response you receive is that you talk 25 percent of the time, and they talk 75 percent.

From this moment on, when you hear a response to your ask, and you do not know what is exactly is on the mind of the person you just asked, use this formula. It will dramatically decrease the time to get you an answer because you are working with the person to help resolve what is most pressing on their mind.

75 Percent / 25 Percent Rule

Now that we have taken care of how to handle the response "I have to think about it," how do you handle the rest of them? Hopefully, you've prepared in your list every response you might receive and how to respond to each. My rule for whatever response you receive is that you talk 25 percent of the time, and they talk 75 percent. The way you keep this proportion is by asking good questions. If the proportion goes the other way, with you doing three-quarters of the talking, you will not be able to get to the heart of exactly what the person is thinking. This is where we "overtalk the ask." You begin explaining more about why there is a need for what you want without listening to their thoughts. If you don't know their thoughts, you guess what they are, and you jump in with long and lengthy explanations, qualifications, or negotiations, hoping you will convince the person to say yes.

Victoria and Grant, both divorced for over a year, were introduced by a friend and began dating. They both enjoyed each other's company, going on motorcycle rides, weekend getaways, and exploring their joint love for finding unique art galleries. She shared with Grant many times that while she loved her time with him, her primary focus was on her children. Both sons were still in college, and one son was having a hard time emotionally dealing with the divorce. Grant, however, wanted more. He was recently retired, his married children were older than Victoria's, and Grant simply wanted more of Victoria's time.

If you were Grant, how would you ask Victoria for more time? These personal asks can bring up tons of emotions, from being filled with confidence to feeling totally insecure and fearful of rejection. How Grant asks will make all the difference in the world. That is part 1. Part

2 is how he asks the right questions when she responds to his asking for more time. A really good way Grant could ask would be this:

"Victoria, we have been together now for eight months, and I could not be happier. Every time I see you or hear your voice, I know there is no one else I'd rather spend time with than you. Can we talk about how we can find a way to spend more time together?"

Here are some of the reactions Victoria might give:

- "I told you I can't."
- "I told you my sons are my priority."
- "You don't think we spend enough time now?"
- "What kind of time are we talking about?"
- "For me, the time we have together is perfect."

I can keep adding to the list of potential responses, but let's stick with these for now so that you can see the importance of the 75 Percent / 25 Percent Rule when it comes to saying something to the person's reaction to your ask. Victoria's responses are pretty defensive, some outright angry, which could cause Grant to be harsh and defensive back. Rather than go down that path, this is how Grant can ask good questions and get to the heart of what's behind Victoria's reactions:

- "I told you I can't."
  Yes, you did, and I heard you. Do you foresee a time—say, in a few months or a year—when we may be able to spend more time together?

- "I told you my sons are my priority,"
  Of course, as it should be, and I totally understand. Do you think there are some things I can help you with your sons that I'm not doing now?

- "You don't think we spend enough time now?"

  I love our time together. I just would like more of it. Do you think we could add going for a walk or meeting for coffee once a week?

- "What kind of time are we talking about?"

  How about we look at our calendars and take this month by month to see where we both might find more time for each other? Would that work for you?

- "For me, the time we have together is perfect."

  I understand, but I had to be honest and try. How about we talk about this in a few months and see how we both feel?

Notice that each response Grant gives is a question. That will get Victoria to open up more and allow Grant to fully understand her why. Why is it that she doesn't want to spend more time with him right now? Grant could have gotten very defensive back by saying something like the following:

- "I don't understand why you can't. Your sons are away at college."
- "Are you saying you don't have the time—or that you don't want to spend more time with me?"

I am sure I've made some pretty defensive remarks when someone asked me to do something that made me feel like I was losing myself and my independence, when deep down I was scared to share so much of myself. I of course correct myself now (not always perfectly, I admit) by practicing how to ask a question back in a calm and non-judgmental way. That is the only way two people can fully understand each other when an ask is made.

CHAPTER 8

Laura's Five Laws of Asking—Law 5

Plan Your Next Move at the End of the Ask

Now that you know how to ask for exactly what you want, it's time for my last law: plan your next move at the very end of your ask.

This is where we close the ask meeting, and unless you have heard "Yes, I will do it right now," you will need a next move to get back to your decision maker to keep your ask alive. This appears to be a simple step. Just set up a time to speak or meet again. Watch what happens. Oftentimes, we say something like this:

- "Thank you for your time. I'll get back to you next week with an in-depth report."
- "Thanks for helping me write this college essay. I'd like you to review my final draft. When are you free?"
- "Thank you for agreeing to connect me with your publisher."

What is missing? We can take a lesson from Rule 1: date and time. There is no specific date or time for the next move by you or others who may now be involved in the decision-making. If you do not suggest a specific date and time to speak or meet again, on average it will take you 2.5 weeks of playing phone tag, sending persistent emails, or sending text messages with the appropriate—or, in some cases, inappropriate—emojis to reach the person you just asked. By this time, your ask is old; it's stale. It has lost its energy, and worse, the person you asked probably forgot most of the details you shared when you asked.

> By taking the small step of suggesting a date and time to discuss your ask again, you will have significantly shortened the time it will take to get a definitive answer.

Here is how we fix it so that you plan your next move at the end of your ask:

- "Thank you for your time. I'll get back to you next week with an in-depth report."
  Thank you for your time. I can have the report ready for you next Tuesday, so how about I give you a call two days later, on Thursday at 10:00 a.m., so we can go over it together, and I can answer any questions you may have?

- "Thanks for helping me to write this college essay. I'd like you to review my final version. When are you free?"
  Thanks for helping me to write this college essay. It is due next Friday. Can I come by next Wednesday at 8:00 a.m. before you start work so that you can review my final version?

- "Thank you for agreeing to connect me with your publisher."
  Thank you for agreeing to connect me with your publisher. I'm eager to find the right publisher, so could you email or call her by this Thursday?

Another one of my favorite mantras is "Small steps will have transformational results." As we say in the law, this is exhibit A. By taking the small step of suggesting a date and time to discuss your ask again, you will have significantly shortened the time it will take to get a definitive answer. Now do your suggested date and time always fit within the time frame of person you have asked? Of course not. But they will allow you to discuss at the end of the ask the date and time that is most convenient to meet or speak again. The bottom line is: don't let your ask trail into a calendar abyss. Suggest that date and time to keep your ask flourishing with the promise of a yes.

Takeaways

1. Before you ask, set your foundation. You need *organization* to organize your thoughts to optimize your success, *structure* to secure your stability and strength to make your best choices, and *focus* because where focus goes, success grows.

2. Practice and use Laura's Five Laws of Asking with all the asks you make, not just the big ones.

   □ Law 1: Know exactly what you want, with numbers and dates. Make sure your ask is really an ask and not a just a statement of what you need.

   □ Law 2: Write down fifteen things you think the person will say to your ask and your fifteen responses to each one. Do not take this step in your head. Writing or typing this list will make you more confident.

   □ Law 3: Deliver with confidence; it is time to shine. You may only have one shot at your ask, so make it your best. Stand up every time you ask. Have your eyes focused on the person you are asking if you do your ask live or via a video. Hang a mirror right in front of the place where you do your asks so that your head, shoulders, and entire body are in alignment, giving you the presence of confidence.

   □ Law 4: Clarify what you think you heard. With any response, do not assume or jump to conclusions regarding what the person is thinking about. Ask good questions so that during this time you are talking 25 percent of the time, and they are talking 75 percent. Only then will you truly know what they are thinking about your ask.

   □ Law 5: Plan your next move at the end of the ask. In your

closing remarks, offer a specific date and time when you can speak, meet, or email the person you just asked. This will ensure that your ask does not drop off for weeks, and it will speed up the time it takes to get you the answer you want: yes!

In the next chapter, you will learn how to ask the tough questions. You know that the ask was always in you, and you had that skill as a child. You have discovered what asking type or types you are and how you can use that to your advantage. You've learned how critically important it is to prepare, ensuring that you pay attention to your tone and to listen with presence. You have practiced Laura's Five Laws of Asking with a friend, colleague, or family member. Now, armed with all these new practical skills, you are ready. It is time to dive in and tackle the hard asks, the ones that sometimes seem so much easier to avoid or the ones that we belabor and think about over and over again. Keep breathing. After you read the next chapter, you will have a whole new perspective so that hard asks will no longer hold you back from getting what you need and deserve.

CHAPTER 9

How to Ask the Tough Questions

Every Ask Needs to Be Two Sentences and One Question

Before we jump in and tackle the really hard asks, the ones where we struggle to get the words out, lose sleep at night wondering how the person will react, and think and rethink how and when we will ever feel comfortable and secure enough to make these asks, there is one special formula that I need to share right now. Although I gave you a brief preview about this formula in previous chapters, this is where we need it the most—the moment you make your hard ask. You've done your prep work, worked through all of the Five Laws of Asking, and now your ask needs to be simple, crisp, and clear. Here is the formula: 2S+1Q. Every ask needs to be two sentences and one question. The

> Here is the formula: 2S+1Q. Every ask needs to be two sentences and one question.

directness of this approach is key to your success. Remember that most asks are overasked and overexplained, and quite simply, there is just way too much discussion on your part so that you leave the person wondering, "Now just what is it that I'm supposed to be thinking about?"

2S+1Q. Let's erase overasking the ask by applying this formula to all the hard asks we are about to successfully master.

The Ask for Help: Personal

Kaila was a very successful attorney for one of the nation's largest law firms. All her relatives—her mother, brother, grandmother, aunts, and cousins—lived in New York, but Kaila lived on the West Coast. One day, she got the call that her mother had a severe stroke that hospitalized her, then subsequently placed her in a skilled nursing rehabilitation facility for physical and speech therapy. In time, her mother progressed well, so the facility arranged for her to go back home and continue the therapies. Kaila came to New York to help her mom, to make sure the home health aides were continuing with physical and speech therapy, and to assist with her legal work and with paying her bills. The problem was that none of her relatives felt the same obligation to help. Kaila became emotionally distressed—to the point that it was affecting her health and distracting her from her work. Kaila was not looking for her relatives to be at her mom's house every day. She just wanted them to visit her from time to time and check in with the health aides.

For Kaila, this was simple. Her relatives "should" have known better and "should" have taken on some of the responsibilities right away. She did want to ask them to pitch in, but she assumed that in time, they would. The problem was, they never did.

We begin this chapter with one of the hardest asks: asking for help. Why is it that we don't want to? Over the years, I have heard that people do not want to ask for help because

- it makes them uncomfortable,
- they fear rejection,
- they think it is imposing,
- they think they should be doing it themselves,
- they don't want to be judged,
- it will appear that they didn't try first before asking,
- the person "should" know what is needed and just do it, or
- people will think that they are incompetent, lazy, or needy.

The *Journal of Psychological Science* did a study on two thousand participants comparing the perspective of those asking for help with the perspective of those being asked. The study revealed that the participants asking for help underestimated the willingness of people wanting to help, as well as how good people felt when they were asked.[8]

My simple illustration for underestimating the willingness of people to help is one I do pretty frequently here in the West Village, NYC. I often see a person on the street staring at their cell phone, twirling around and trying to figure out in which direction they should walk. Inevitably they don't ask the people walking by to point them in the right direction. I always walk up to them and ask, "Can I help you?" Even if they say, "No, I'm good," they always say it with a smile. I know they appreciate that someone wants to point them in the right direction. I feel good because I didn't walk away, pretending that I didn't see them or didn't care enough to offer assistance. The

---

8   Catherine Pearson, "Go Ahead, Ask for Help—People Are Happy to Give It," *New York Times*, September 2022, accessed February 15, 2023, https://www.nytimes.com/2022/09/15/well/family/asking-for-help.html.

best reward is when I ask them if they need help, and they say, "Yes. Can you tell me how to get to the Path Train?" Usually, the Path Train is no more than a half block from where they are standing. I feel that I've helped them make their life a little less complicated, and I've saved them time.

For Kaila, this ask for help has a lot of emotional family issues, which makes this a hard ask. Oftentimes, it is not easy to separate past experiences, conversations, and confrontations from the present time, when you want a family member to do something that is very important to you. In this example, it is not simply the act of picking up the phone and, in the middle of a catch-up call, stating that you need them to share the responsibilities. I understand that 100 percent. My question for anyone in Kaila's position, in which other people, particularly family members, can take on some of the responsibilities, is this: "Is it worth risking your emotional and physical health and possibly jeopardizing your productivity at work just because you don't want to ask or feel that people should just do the right thing?" My recommendation on how to make this hard ask easier follows. First, I would select the family member who lives closest to the mom and has some time to check in on her. In this case, it was Kaila's brother. Next, I would ask him in this way, using two sentences and a question (2S+1Q), preferably doing the ask in person:

"[Use the brother's first name], I know you have—and we all have, as a family—gone through a lot with Mom's stroke, hospitalization, and rehab facility, and now she is home. While I have come back for as long as I can to take care of her legal needs and check in with the health aides, I need to go back home because work does require me to be physically in the office three days a week. Can we put together a plan where we all can share some responsibility for her care going forward?"

My advice for asking for help is to always recognize, acknowledge, and (in some instances) empathize with the person you are asking. Next, get to what you have done so far and your why—Why do you need help? At the end, you ask how you can solve it together. If you can solve an ask for help together, the person will be more apt to hear you out and not be so defensive. Notice that I did not recommend that Kaila use what can be interpreted as harsh words, which can lead to a harsh tone such as these:

- "Well, I've been here for three weeks, and I thought the family would come by so that we can figure out what's best for Mom."
- "The health aides are doing as much as they can, but we all need to stop by and check on them."
- "You all know that I can't be here longer, and you all do live closer, so can you just coordinate when you can see her and check on the aides?"

Another way not to ask for help is to come across too apologetic right from the start. Kaila could have said:

"I know how superbusy you are, and if you can't do this, well, OK. Right now, Mom needs someone to check in with her from time to time just to make sure she is keeping the progress with her therapies. It's no big deal if you can't, but do you think you could drop by a few times a week?"

I have a ritual each morning; I like to read a real newspaper. I'm sparing my eyes from what I know lies ahead of me each day, working on a computer screen. As a former journalist, I just love the feel of a real newspaper, and I absorb the news story more when I read it in my hands and not online. One morning I was reading a section title "Here to Help." The story line was "Go Ahead and Ask for Help—People Are Happy to Give It." Now this is my kind of story. The article asked

Lizzie Post, a copresident of the Emily Post Institute, how a daughter should ask her mother to watch the grandchildren for several days. I'm thinking, *This is a great ask, and like Kaila, it involves an ask of a family member for help.* As I kept reading, I got infuriated. First, it said that it is recommended to give a person an "out" right up front for a bigger request. Next, the suggestion was that the daughter say, "Hey, Mom, it would be great if you can, but no pressure if you can't. We will be able to find someone else."[9]

Now I'm thinking, *With advice like this, there is truly not enough of me to go around!* This way to ask is so wrong in so many ways. Your exercise right now is to list what is so wrong with the way the article suggested the daughter ask her mother for help watching the kids. How would you have asked for help?

> If your mindset is that you need to give a person an "out" before you ask, then why are you making this ask in the first place?

First, if your mindset is that you need to give a person an "out" before you ask, then why are you making this ask in the first place? Second, giving that person an immediate way out using the language "No pressure if you can't" should never be part of the initial ask. Third, in this case, it is telling the grandmother that the daughter has plan B, plan C, and possibly plan D if she can't watch the grandchildren. Imagine how this grandmother feels with this kind of ask for help. I'm guessing that the grandmother does not feel important because she's been told that others can do it. It is never helpful to give a person on "out" when you ask, regardless of the size or magnitude of your ask. The way to ask for this kind of help is this:

---

9   Ibid.

"Mom, as luck would have it, I have to be out of town for a few days next week, specifically Tuesday through Friday. I'd love for you to watch the kids, and I will make sure you have everything you need so that this does not interfere with your schedule. Is this OK with you?"

Remember, it is so important to give the person you are asking the breathing room to hear their thoughts after you ask, and the way you do so is to end with an open-ended question: "Is this OK with you?" or "Will this work for you?" or "Do you have any concerns?"

The Ask for Help: Career

The ask for help is not always for a personal need. It surfaces many times in our professional lives, our careers. Hard asks for career help can be to meet one of the following needs:

- Contact an industry leader to be a mentor
- Secure a new board member
- Ask for a raise
- Get a coworker to do their share of the work on a joint project
- Approach a boss when you are swamped with work
- Work from home full time
- Be promoted to the next-level position
- Act as the lead on a case with a client
- Find the right study group to pass an important certification exam
- Negotiate a higher client fee
- Get a client referral
- Receive more training for your staff
- Set realistic timelines to achieve your goals
- Be given more vacation time

If you need to ask for something that affects your career, prepare your ask in the way that we covered in chapter 3, and apply the Five Laws of Asking that we covered in chapters 4 through 8 to each situation. Particularly when it comes to something that is vital to your profession, I'm reinforcing the need to adhere strictly to Law 1: be sure to include a specific amount and specific date. When I was managing large staffs at Temple University and Pace University, I cannot tell you how many times people would walk into my office and say something like the following:

- "I need a raise."
- "I need more vacation time."
- "I want to be considered for the open director position."
- "I want my staff to go to this conference."
- "We need more board members who can make significant gifts."
- "Can we adjust my goals?"
- "The marketing team won't produce our appeals on time."

It is way easier to "say" these things to the decision maker than it is to take the time and map out exactly what you want, with numbers and dates. The consequences of your not taking the time to think out the exact number and the exact date will always lead you down the path of not getting it at all.

Using the 2S+1Q formula, at the moment of your ask, you can make the hard asks easy for your career needs:

- **Contact an industry leader to be a mentor**
  You have been so helpful and so generous with your time. I think you have a great idea of reaching out to Natalie, the CFO, and asking her if she would meet with me and then possibly serve as my mentor. Do you think you could email

her by next Tuesday and ask her if she would take the time to meet with me?

- **Secure a new board member**

  Amani, thank you for serving on our marketing committee. Your outside expertise has really helped our organization build a better brand and awareness in the community. Would you consider now joining us as a board member?

> The consequences of your not taking the time to think out the exact number and the exact date will always lead you down the path of not getting it at all.

- **Ask for a raise (a personal favorite of mine!)**

  Briana, thank you for trusting me to be the head of our new product development team. I'm asking you now for a $15,000 raise effective January 1 of next year. How can I help you reach this important decision?

- **Get a coworker to do their share of the work on a joint project**

  Jackson, we both have a deadline of next Wednesday to have a draft of our plans for the new HVAC system in the gymnasium. I've completed my portion. Do you think you can complete yours by this Friday so that we will have next Monday and Tuesday to make our final revisions before we send this in on Wednesday?

- **Approach a boss when you are swamped with work**

  Mia, I rarely do this, as you know, but right now I am finding it extremely difficult to make all my deliveries by 6:00 p.m. I'd like to go over our workflow chart with you because I think I've found a way where we can shift a few things around and still keep our customers satisfied. Can we go over that now?

- **Work from home full time**

  Aiden, as you know, for the past two years our team has worked from home, and we have not missed a deadline. I feel that we are so much more productive, so much more creative, and so much happier when we work from home. Will you consider letting us all work for home through the end of next year?

- **Be promoted to the next-level position**

  Tess, I'd like to talk to you about promoting me by the end of this month to an assistant vice president. I have brought with me a written plan on how I can fulfill the current job requirements as well as some suggested ways I can bring some new skills to this position. Can I go over the details with you?

- **Act as the lead on a case with a client**

  Hudson, it is fantastic that the firm just secured the product liability case from a new client. Product liability is my specialty, and I want to be the lead attorney on this case. The team is ready to get started, so do I have your permission now to take the lead on this case?

- **Find the right study group to pass an important certification exam**

  Professor, passing this exam is so important to me, and I know I could use the help of a study group to keep me focused. I'm looking to join one by next Monday. Do you have any suggestions or recommendations of a study group, either in person or online, where you feel I would fit best?

- **Negotiate a higher client fee**

  Avery, you've been a great client this past year, and I hope our accounting services have helped your company's cash flow. The firm is raising its rates at the first of the year, and for you and your company, with the same services we have been providing, it would raise your monthly retainer by $500 each month. Do you have any questions for me?

- **Get a client referral**

  Ryan, I hope that you and your wife are truly excited and satisfied with the renovations we did in your backyard, building a new pool, and creating a brand-new area for you to be able to cook outside and enjoy your company. Our next customer comes from our last customer. Would you be willing to speak with a potential customer next Wednesday about the work we completed in your backyard?

- **Receive more training for your staff**

  Leah, our ten new hires could add extra skill sets for the company if they could receive outside training. I found a two-day conference that our new hires could go to on May 1 that would cost $5,000 for the ten of us. Can I have your permission for them to go?

- **Set realistic timelines to achieve your goals**

  Hunter, right now I am tasked to visit with fifteen prospects or donors a month. Over the past eight months, I've made fifty calls a month and backed them up with emails, and I have been able to visit with ten prospects or donors. Can we agree that we need to readjust my goal to do ten visits per month so that I will be eligible for my bonus in December?

- **Be given more vacation time**

  Hailey, I've been with the company now for over four years and have always looked forward to my two-week vacation. This summer my family and I are planning a long trip to Europe, as our daughter will be doing an internship in Barcelona. Can I have one additional week of vacation in addition to my two weeks this summer?

The Ask Is a Conversation, Not a Confrontation

Once you realize that the ask is a conversation, an exchange of ideas, the ask becomes effortless.

These suggested ways to ask using 2S+1Q all have an additional benefit for you. By ending your ask with a question, you are not only inviting the person to respond while you listen, but you are also inviting more discussion. Look at the example above in asking to secure a new board member. It ends with "Would you consider now joining us as a board member?" The person is not going to say yes or no on the spot. The person is going to say something like this:

- "Tell me more. What does that entail?"
- "Do you have the roles and responsibilities for board members that you can share with me?"
- "How much do I have to give each year?"
- "How many board members do you have?"
- "How many meetings do I have to attend?"

While we all want to hear yes on the spot, if that is your sole focus, you will begin to look and sound defensive or disappointed when you hear anything but a yes. What you really want is the opportunity to have an open conversation about what you need. This is where you will have the chance to answer any and all questions they may have. Remember you probably can anticipate their questions if you did Law 2 ("Write down fifteen things you think the person will say to your ask") ahead of asking. Once you realize that the ask is a conversation, an exchange of ideas, the ask becomes effortless.

How They Treat the Process Is How You Will Be Treated

While you practice your asks for your career from time to time throughout your life, please keep this one very important mantra in mind: how they treat the process is how you will be treated. I learned this the hard way, and I wish I had learned it sooner. When I first started working at a university, I worked my way up from director of major gifts, to senior director of major gifts, to assistant vice president (AVP). With each promotion, I received more responsibility, and I was paid more and earned more vacation time. While I was the AVP, we had a change in leadership. My new boss came in, and instead of having the responsibility of raising money for six schools and colleges, I was now responsible for fifteen schools and colleges, the athletic program, and two hospitals. The other AVP had marketing and communications, research, and corporate and foundation relations. This was clearly an uneven division of labor. The worst part was that the other AVP was making more than I, even though I had much more responsibility.

I went in, and I must say, I did a pretty good ask for a raise for the amount that would be on par with the other AVP. He said no. He told me the other AVP had been at the university longer than I, and she should be paid more, regardless of the work division. Needless to say, I was not happy, but I hunkered down, raising money and managing a staff of forty. My boss would come to all my meetings with the deans and department heads of the fifteen schools and colleges, the executive directors of the two hospitals, and the head and assistant head of the athletic program, where we worked out next steps of whom we needed to engage and then ask for money. After we walked out of those meetings, all the work always fell on me. Fortunately for me, two years later, I was offered the vice president position at another university and left. Years later, I looked back on that experience and wondered why I didn't see it then, but I could see it now. During your career ask, watch carefully how you are treated. If you felt it was unfair or unkind, or that you never really received a full explanation, or the one you received seemed extremely dubious to you, your work life is not going to get much better after your ask. I've seen this time after time— people coming to me while they are job seeking or asking for that raise and promotion, and the decision makers are really unfairly screwing up this process. They do not miraculously change their demeanors, indecisiveness, tones, or words once a decision is made, even if it is made in your favor. My big advice is that you pay attention to this process because that is how your work life is headed after your career ask. How they treat the process is how they will treat you.

The Ask for Money

"When you ask for money, you are not taking something away; you are giving an opportunity."

This is one of my all-time favorite mantras, which I made up many years ago. I share this with anyone who truly wants and needs to ask for money but can't get the words out. Many people have shared with me that when they think of asking someone for money, they visualize dollar bills flying out of people's pockets, ATMs, or retirement accounts and taking money away from their family's travel, enjoyment, faith, creative projects, health, and education. I understand why people would feel this way. Money affects us all, at all stages in our lives. It has the power to enhance and boost our lives, or it can hinder and impede our happiness and lifestyles. I call it an "emotional firecracker." When things are good monetarily, and you feel that you are in a good financial state, life is good. When you've just paid your bills online and thought you'd have a lot more left, or a friend calls you to go to dinner, and you know she drinks only the best champagne that you cannot afford, your money emotions are triggered. The firecracker goes off and leaves you crashing to the ground.

Taking this a step further, money affects your health and your lifestyle. Adults who are stressed about their personal finances are twice as likely to die following a heart attack than those who do not worry about money.[10] In addition to your health, money can also wreak havoc in your personal life. Ramsey Solutions conducted a study of one thousand adults to gain a better understanding of how couples communicate about their finances. In addition to finding out that the number-one reason couples argue is money, here are some eye openers:[11]

- Nearly two-thirds of all marriages start off in debt.
- One-third of people who said they argued with their spouse about money hid purchases from their spouses.
- Ninety-four percent who said they had a great marriage discussed their money dreams with their spouses.
- Sixty-three percent who are carrying $50,000 or more in debt felt anxious talking about their personal finances.

---

10   Jason R. Falvey, Alexandra M. Hajduk, Christopher R. Keys, "Association of Financial Strain With Mortality Among Older US Adults Recovering From an Acute Myocardial Infarction," *JAMA Internal Medicine*, February 2022, accessed February 15, 2023, doi:10.1080/01634372.2021.195366 2.

11   Ramsey Solutions, "Money Ruining Marriages in America: A Ramsey Solutions Study," Ramsey Solutions, February 2018, accessed February 15, 2023, https://www.ramseysolutions.com/company/newsroom/releases/money-ruining-marriages-in-america.

Asking for money is one of the most common asks because any ask you make has a monetary implication. When you ask for money, your feelings, your experiences, and your finances come up. Consider the following list of what money can mean, and you will have a pretty good idea that money is embedded in very ask you make. Money can do the following:

- Define your stature in life.
- Determine your success (or lack of success).
- Be the reason you stick with your job.
- Be why you need to work and why you work where you do.
- Determine when and whether you retire.
- Be a factor in when and where your children or grandchildren go to school.
- Set the limits of what you give to your family during your lifetime or through your will.
- Be the deciding factor in where you live and where you have a vacation home.
- Determine how much you can give to charity.
- Make you reflect on whether you made the right choices in your life.
- Govern how much you will inherit.
- Govern how much you borrow.
- Govern how much you save.
- Govern how much can invest.
- Determine how much you can spend each day, week, and month.
- Be a factor in selecting your healthcare coverage and the number of doctor visits and surgeries.
- Be the source of arguments, tension, and unspoken resentment.
- Cause you to gain or lose weight.

- Keep you from being spiritually connected.
- Keep you up at night.

As I mentioned earlier, when you ask for money, your emotional firecracker is ignited, and you think, "If I don't have that much, how can I ask for that much?" or "This is pretty bold of me; maybe I should ask for less," or "If I bring up paying the bills, we'll just get into another argument." My job is to have you move beyond this emotional tension, the anxiety, and the apprehension by showing you how you can make the money ask that is comfortable for you and the person you asking. This is why you must first embrace the mindset that when you ask for money, you are giving an opportunity. Once you do, you will be able to make any ask for money a bit easier. Please do not pretend or convince yourself that it does not come up because it does. When it does, I need you to do a visualization. Visualize a door, one that is special for you. It could be a French double door overlooking acres of gardens, a Victorian door with the finest hand-carved mahogany, or something quite modern with bold, brilliant color and design. Now every time you need to ask for money, visualize that door swinging open and yourself walking through the archway of that magnificent door. You are embarking on an opportunity that you want to share with someone. It is an open opportunity, an open door, to give someone the opportunity to want to hear your ask.

> It is an open opportunity, an open door, to give someone the opportunity to want to hear your ask.

Investment Ask

Maddy is a dynamic twenty-one-year-old with a burgeoning new fashion start-up company. When I asked her how much money her

109

company needs, she said "One-point-two million." It was fantastic that she knew the amount, but I asked: How did she come up with that number? She hesitated at first and then realized that unless she had the complete breakdown of costs and expenses and when she needed a cash investment, no one would invest in her business. If you have ever watched an episode of Shark Tank, you know that any investor will ask you right off the top for these facts. Law 1: Know exactly what you want, with numbers and dates. In this case Maddy's business plan needed a detailed budget, sales projections, and a timeline.

Then I asked her who she was going to ask for this funding and how much she was going to ask each person to invest. She said she only had one person in mind, her mentor, but of course she couldn't ask him. Before we addressed that issue, I shared with her that everyone needs to have this model when they are seeking money outright:

Make a written list of people and entities that are aligned with your business, your organization, and your needs. Ask them in priority order, starting with people and entities that have the potential to give you the biggest amount in the quickest amount of time.

By "entities," I mean companies and foundations. I thought Maddy would then skip over her mentor and that she would start listing with me other people like relatives, but she didn't. She said that her mentor had done very well, not only in the fashion industry but in other business investments as well. Knowing this fact, I told her he was the absolute best person to ask first.

We went over fifteen things her mentor could say and the responses she could give him to each, and we recorded her voice so that she had the right tone to deliver her ask. Now it was time to craft her ask. This is what I suggested she say to him:

"You have been my mentor for the past three years, and you above anyone else know that opening a new line takes a major investment. While I was nervous and uncomfortable because I would never want to jeopardize our relationship and all you have taught me, I am confident now that you are the perfect person to be the first to invest in my work. Will you consider making an investment of $500,000, payable over the next eight months, so that I can launch my dream project?"

He replied that he was wondering if she was going to ask him and said that he would need to pay it out over two years instead of eight months. Needless to say, Maddy was over the moon and filled with joy.

There are three very important lessons to this story for anyone who needs to ask for money, whether that be for a business, charity, or for yourself. First, you do need to think carefully of who is aligned with what you do and would be willing to support your business, your charity, or you. The tendency is always to consider who has the most assets, who is the most successful businessperson, or who is the biggest supporter of charities. If those people who fulfill those criteria have little or no interest in what you do or what your opportunity for them will be, why would you ask them? The hope is of course that you or your unique business or charity will be so appealing that you can win them over to say yes to you. There are perfect examples of this in the nonprofit sector with so many groups going after Elon Musk, Gautam Adani, Mackenzie Scott, Warren Buffet, Richard Branson, George Bezos, or Larry Ellison for money because, after all, these people have either built dynasty businesses, or they are known to give great amounts to nonprofits. If your nonprofit is not what they fund or is not of interest to them, or they have no idea what your charity does, asking them for money at this stage will fall into a black hole.

> People will give to you if they know, like, and trust you.

Second, take this list of people and entities who are aligned with what you do or who you are, and prioritize them by who knows, likes, and trusts you the most. I come back to this simple rule: people will give to you if they know, like, and trust you. So simple yet so powerful and true. One of my marketing agents, Lisa Marie, whom I've known for years, reached out to me and asked me to go online and support her daughter's first dance recital. The child who raised the most money would win a prize. I'm not normally a fan of supporting or sponsoring runs, bicycle races, bake sales, because when I give, I make significant gifts to select charities that I have either volunteered with or feel passionate about the impact they are making on people's lives. I could not turn this one down because over the years, Lisa Marie and I both knew, liked, and trusted each other implicitly. I made her a list of people she needed to ask. A bonus for me was that her daughter at the young age of four is learning about fundraising, so how could I say no?

> People leave clues; we miss every one of them. My mantra here fits perfectly in this section because if you do not go over prior conversations and communications, you are apt to be blindsided when you ask for money.

Third, now that you have your priority list, see who has the most assets and can do it in the quickest time. Embedded in my advice is a two-part process, which is easy to skip over, especially when asking for investment money. Part 1 is that you have to determine who has the assets to fund your investment at the higher levels. Part 2 goes to the timing of when they can do it. Since these are people you know, like, and trust, think back on conversations you've had or emails you have exchanged for each person on your list. What financial state are they in right now? Are their businesses expanding, thriving, or struggling? Have they personally committed to investing in their own families? Are they taking a year or two off on a sabbatical, contemplating retirement, or suddenly strapped with unforeseen expenses? People leave clues; we miss every one of them. My mantra here fits perfectly in this section because if you do not go over prior conversations and communications, you are apt to be blindsided when you ask for money. The person will look at you and say, "But you know I shared with you I just put most of my assets in expanding the business" or "I believe you know I'm about to retire" or "You know that I've brought on a few younger partners, and we are going to take some time to revamp our business model." Don't miss a clue they have shared with you. Spend the time to go over what each person has said to you in the months prior to your ask.

A word of caution here: I am by no means making the assumption that anyone who is going through these situations should not be on your investment ask list or that they automatically fall to the bottom. I am stating that, like Law 2, you need to be prepared that any one of these circumstances may come up when you ask, so you have to be ready for them. In the prioritization of your investment ask list, if you have people or entities that are doing very well or have shared with you directly or indirectly their financial stability and success, then they should go to the top of your list.

Asking people in priority order is so important when asking for money for any purpose. Maddy had to ask her mentor because he was guiding her to this point of her creative career, and he had the assets to invest in her. If she did not ask him first, what do you think he would have said, or how do you think he would have felt, when he heard or knew that she had asked others before him? Pretty lousy. Don't misjudge the importance of primacy in asking.

The Return-My-Money Ask

Do you have a friend who is the nicest, kindest, funniest, most personable, always-there-for-you, purehearted person? That person for me is Nancy, whom I met in my second year of college. We lived on the same floor in Alan Dormitory at Rutgers College in New Jersey. During the winter of the year we met, the entire floor came down with the flu. There was Nancy, with a face cloth soaked in rubbing alcohol, placing it on everyone's forehead to break our fevers while she had pancakes for all of us cooking in her electric frying pan—which of course she was not supposed to have in our dorm.

Nancy and I have stayed good friends over these many years, and I came to learn that her kindheartedness was being taken advantage of. Steve was one of her son's friends who, through some family drama, wound up with no place to live. Nancy's son asked if Steve could come and live with them for two weeks while he tried to look for a place to live. The two weeks turned into two years. Nancy did not mind, as she grew closer to Steve, and since Steve did not have a mother, he called Nancy "Mom." Nancy had three sons, and she called Steve her fourth.

Steve started dating Monica, and now that he had a good job, he decided to find a place so that he and Monica could live together. He found an apartment, but it required a $2,400 deposit. Steve didn't have this amount saved, so he asked Nancy for the money. Nancy gave it to him on the condition that it was an interest-free loan to be paid back within six months. Steve honored her terms, and within six months, he paid back the money in full.

Nancy had not seen Steve for a while until she received a call from him asking if they could catch up and meet for breakfast. At the breakfast meeting, Steve did it again. He asked Nancy this time for $8,000 so that he could buy a delivery truck business from a friend. Thinking this would really help him become stable in a business, she gave him the money, again as an interest-free loan. But at the time, she never said when she wanted the money back. Now years have gone by, and Nancy still does not have her $8,000. To add to the hurt and disappointment, she has seen Steve post Facebook pictures of his vacations.

Asking for money back from someone you know, love, and trust (or, at the time you loaned the money, trusted) is a hard ask. My good friend Nancy felt that in time he would come around, do the right thing, and pay it back without her needing to ask. She fell into the trap of one of our three devils, time: "In time he will have the money to pay me back," "If I give him more time, he will save enough from his new business and pay me back," or "In time I will get a check in the mail from him."

So I told Nancy it was time to confront Steve, and when she did, I suggested she say this:

"Steve, you really hurt me and disappointed me that it has been over two years, and you have not paid me back the $8,000 I loaned you. I am asking you now to pay me back with either cash or a certified check by March 1 of this year, or I will contact my attorney. Do you understand my terms?"

It is important that you let out your hurt, disappointment, and anger in your ask, as suggested in the first sentence of Nancy's ask. As we talked about in chapter 3, be careful of your tone in the delivery of your ask. An angry, loud, harsh voice can escalate to a confrontation. What is the real goal here? To unload on Steve, to tell him what a loser he is? No. It is important that you keep your eyes on the prize, and that is the goal. I like to say: "What is the goal? And work backward." Nancy's goal is to get her $8,000 back. How can she do it best? Make a direct, firm (this is her tone), specific ask with an exact amount and date. That is it. Mission accomplished.

I also suggested that she put this in writing, sign and date it, make a copy, and give it to him. A written, signed document spelling out the specific terms serves as a contract, and if it is broken, there will be consequences. If Steve does not come through by March 1, she has her backup plan to seek legal enforcement.

The Charitable Ask

She had the world of asking in the palm of her hand. She was dynamic, sincere, personable, well respected, poised, and passionate, and she was a preparation machine. Her asking track record was stellar. The only thing missing was this: she could not ask her friends for money.

Kristen was an executive board member and chair of the fundraising committee for a global food bank organization that was in the middle of a $100 million campaign during its celebratory fiftieth anniversary year. Her daughter was best friends with a girl at school whose father, Ari, was extremely wealthy. Ari made his money in international finance. Kristen knew Ari well because their girls had many playdates together. Over occasional coffee meetings, he asked Kristen about her board service. She shared how dedicated she was to the organization's mission and how important it was to reduce food waste and to defeat world hunger by partnering with other organizations to create new, sustainable foodbanks. She explained how the scarcity of food can have a ripple effort on a family, a community, and a country's economic and social stability.

He was very interested and asked detailed questions about the organization's direct and indirect costs; how much they raised to date and from what sources; the number of families, particularly children, they served; the number of food banks they created; and the countries they served. Kristen asked him an important question: Why was it particularly important for him to know about the number of families and particularly children they served? He got quiet, looked down, and said that he was from India, and growing up during hard times, food had not always been available to him. He could identify with what these families, particularly the children, were going through. At that moment, Kristen asked him if he'd like to know more about the organization and perhaps in time get involved or volunteer. He said he'd love to know more, but his time was limited. Over the next several months, Kristen set up a brief meeting for him to meet with the CEO of the organization and Skype meetings to speak with some of the families and children who had benefited from the organization.

Kristen did everything any terrific fundraiser would do: invite, engage, and educate a person about the nonprofit, and the next step was to ask for money. Her biggest stumbling block surfaced. She knew him and was afraid to ask him for money because it might sabotage their relationship and maybe the friendship between their daughters. Still, she didn't want to give up the opportunity to ask him. She just didn't know how she could do it. This is such a common issue when you have people who are close to you, such as friends, colleagues, and family members, and they know, like, and trust you, plus they have the means to make the gift. You think by making an ask, the whole relationship will fall to pieces, that they will be angry or annoyed that you crossed a line in your relationship, or worse, that they won't speak to you again.

At their next coffee meeting, Ari asked her how the fundraising was going and what the organization needed. Kristen was surprised at first by his question and somehow managed to say, "What we need is money." He asked how much, and while Kristen couldn't figure out the exact amount on the spot, she did ask him, "Would you like to donate?"

While this story has a happy and successful ending, I wanted to show that with a bit more preparation and drawing upon Laws 1 and 2, anyone who needs to ask for a charitable gift—whether the person is a close friend or someone you are getting to know because they may be a supporter for the nonprofit—can make the ask easier. First, while you are engaging and conversing about the work of the organization as well as the work you are doing for the nonprofit, listen for clues. In this case, what deeply touched Ari was the work this organization was doing to stop hunger, particularly with children, because he had experienced hunger as a child. When you hear something like this, you need to incorporate it in your ask. Second, be thinking about the amount of money you want to ask for and when you'd like the person to make the gift during the time period that you are in discussion with them about the nonprofit. In this case, Ari jumped the gun and asked her what she needed. Had she been thinking about this ahead of time, she would have been able to give him an amount she had in mind. As you know, Law 1 also requires you to give the person the specifics of the timeline. If Kristen had $100,000 in mind for Ari, well, what time period did she have in mind for him to do it? One year, three years, five years, or more? Third, if it is a close friend, relative or colleague, and you are worried that the person may feel you are taking advantage of them because you know them so well (hence, that is how you got to the ask amount), be honest and admit it. There is no sense in ignoring it or pretending it doesn't matter to you. The ask could have been done the following way:

"I must admit this is a bit awkward, and I am a bit uncomfortable, as I am not used to asking friends, especially a good friend like you. Ari, I heard you say how important our work is to you because you experienced hunger as a child. Would you consider a gift of $100,000 that you can do over the next three years, so that together we can ensure that our global efforts are successful to provide the food our children and their families need?"

If this is too direct for you, and you feel you can't or really don't want to ask someone close to you for money, then try this. During one of your conversations, say:

"You know how involved I am with this charity and that part of my role is to raise money. I have no idea whether you are interested in getting more involved with us and possibly supporting as at some time. Is this something that interests you?"

It is my plan B for you because I totally understand and have been there when it just doesn't feel right to ask for a specific amount early on from someone who knows you very well. Over the years, I have asked many board members, committee members, and volunteers at nonprofits if they feel more comfortable asking someone they know very well, someone they know a little, or someone they don't know at all for money. The great majority of people say they'd rather ask someone they know just a little or not at all. In order to make sure that your "close" people are asked and not neglected just because they are close, I always

> If you are raising money for a charity, and your close friends, family, and colleagues know that you are raising money, if you do not ask them, they feel that there is this group of people who are richer, smarter, and better than they, and they are not in it.

encourage you to embrace this mindset, as it may serve as a motivator for you. If you are raising money for a charity, and your close friends, family, and colleagues know that you are raising money, if you do not ask them, they feel that there is this group of people who are richer, smarter, and better than they, and they are not in it. It's true. Many people have said to me: "Why didn't they ask me?" or "I guess they thought I wouldn't be interested" or "I'm sure they have their wealthy people to go to."

My hope is that plan B will be a stepping stone for you to feel more comfortable and more confident to ask people who are close to you. When you make this type of ask, it is an invitation, nothing more. Then you just need to sit back and listen to the response. If the person says, "Sure. What did you have in mind?" then you have the open lane to make your ask. If they say, "I'm involved with other groups" then say: "Thank you for your honesty. Can I let you know from time to time how we are doing?" This way, you leave the door open so that maybe in the future, the person may be interested and may be willing to hear about your ask.

The Ask Meeting: Always Let the Person Know It's Not Just Coffee

An important part of the ask is setting up the ask meeting. Like our example with Kristen, when she wants to ask Ari for money, she should set up a meeting over coffee, as they had done in the past, and be clear that she wants to discuss an opportunity she has for him. Make sure the person has some idea that it won't be just coffee and discussing schools, children, and life. Think of yourself enjoying a great cappuccino when a friend blurts out that they want you to consider giving money. It's jarring, it's inconsiderate, and above all, it may put a damper on your relationship. You do not have to say you will be asking the person for money when you set up the ask meeting, but you should let them know that you have an opportunity for them. This will benefit you for several reasons:

1. If they keep putting off the meeting or simply don't have the time to meet you, then it is not the right time to ask them.

2. If they press you to tell them over the phone, texting or emailing, "What's this all about?" tell them it is important to you that you discuss it in person.

3. If they ask, "Is this about money?" I say honesty wins the day, so use some humor and say, "What topic in life isn't about money?" Then follow up with, "Yes it is, but there is so much more, and I'd like the opportunity to share this with you in person."

Add or Subtract the Zeros—the Ask Is the Same

Whether you are asking for $30, $500, $100,000, $1 million—or more—your ask is the same. That is a hard concept to grasp at first because you think, Shouldn't the magnitude of the amount govern a much different process than if I were to ask for a lower amount? The answer is no. First, any ask, especially for money, requires you to stick to the ask formula: two sentences and a question. Second, your goal for any monetary ask is to have the person have a crystal-clear idea of exactly what it is you are asking them, whether that be a small, medium or jumbo amount. Is there more anxiety asking for a larger amount? Well, sometimes, but we can be just as nervous asking a friend to buy a few boxes of Girl Scout Cookies as we can asking them to spend five figures for a table for your charity's gala. This is where the simple ask formula can turn that hard ask into an easy one. Do not think that the size of ask dictates a different approach. If you do, then you will have multiple ways you feel you will need to memorize when you ask for different amounts. Let's make your life easy by applying one formula to all your money asks. The best part of all? It works. The next time your children are raising money for a sports team, bake sale, or dance recital, use the ask formula. The next time you need to ask someone to support a charity's fundraiser, campaign, or event, use the ask formula. You will soon feel so much lighter and at ease because you have one path, one way, to make a terrific ask.[12]

The Ask for Health

The Medical-Procedure Ask

My mother was propped up high on her fluffy pillows with lots of warm blankets, surrounded by her universe of white sheets. As she is eighty-seven years old and 104 pounds at most, her tiny bones got pretty cold in the antiseptic, keep-it-as-cold-as-you-can hospital room. Having made it through a heart attack in her forties, with several stents keeping her vital organ working, she needed a procedure called a thoracic endovascular aortic repair to keep her alive. It would require cutting a small area at the top of her leg to insert guide wires carrying a replacement valve to seal up the aneurysm. If the procedure was not done, there would not be enough blood pumping through her aorta to her heart.

The surgeon and his attending physician entered her room. The surgeon started flipping through his clipboard of thick white paper with lots of black-and-white graphs. By the look on his face and the gaze in his eyes, my mother knew there was a problem. He said that looking over her charts, he saw she had a lot of calcium deposits where the guide wires had to make their way to place the stent. There was the possibility the stent could not make it all the way to her aorta. That's when I lost it:

"Why are you telling us this now?" I demanded. ""What are the risks if you get halfway through, and you can't do the whole thing?

---

12   For more examples and tips on business asks and philanthropy asks, see Laura Fredricks, *THE ASK: For Business, For Philanthropy, For Everyday Living* (New Jersey: Wiley, 2018).

Are you still going through with this? You can't tell me you just found out about these calcium deposits."

When you mess with my mother's health, I come out fighting.

Using her scrawny little elbows, Mom propped herself up. She had every emotion circling in her face: confusion, anger, and worse, depression. All she could say was "What does this mean?" over and over again. The surgeon said he had to let us know that the calcium deposits might hinder the procedure, but they were going forward with the surgery as planned. Hours later, when Mom was coming out of her anesthesia in the recovery room, the attending physician came in. She looked really happy with a big smile, and now she was carrying the clipboard. She said while they could not get to the valve area to repair the leak, they were able to reduce the amount of calcium surrounding the heart area with the guide wires. If Mom had any strength in her, I thought she would leap up and smack her. Instead she lay still with an exhausted look of disgust. All she could say was "Now what?"

In that moment, I knew what we did wrong. I never asked these hard questions up front. We often take for granted that the doctors will let us know of any warning signs, complications, or trouble areas way before the day of surgery. Sometimes they do; sometimes they don't. When it comes to your health or the health of a loved one, asking up front and being proactive with your asks will be your biggest emotional asset. It will be the armor you need to protect yourself from sudden and unexpected, heart-wrenching medical news.

Here is what I should have said when Mom was meeting with the doctors prior to her surgery: "You know my mom is eighty-seven years old with a history of heart disease. Without this procedure, her heart will continue to weaken, and there could be fatal consequences." And here are the questions I should have asked:

1. "How many eighty-seven-year-old or older patients have you performed this procedure on?"
2. "What is your track record of success with this procedure?"
3. "Is there any alternative if the surgery does not go well?"
4. "What have other patients experienced when the surgery could not be performed?"
5. "Can you walk me through exactly how you will be doing this?"
6. "With her present condition, do you have any concerns?"
7. "What equipment are you using, and who manufactures it?"
8. "Does she need to be tested for possible reaction she may have to the equipment, anesthesia, or medication she will need during this procedure?"

We don't think clearly when stressful health issues arise because our anxiety soaks up many or our mental resources. Some call this "brain fog."[13]

When you are faced with anything health related for which you have to make decisions, my suggestion is to first do your outside research, and then, when you are in the initial discussions with your doctor, write down the questions you want to ask. Frankly, I can't see my way out of a paper bag when health decisions need to be made on the spot or come up as a surprise. I now make a list and keep adding to the list as I think of things. That will help me make a rational decision, and I will not beat myself up, as I did with Mom when I should have asked those questions way before the day of her surgery.

---

13   Yalda Safai and Zawn Villines, "What to Know about Anxiety and Brain Fog," MedicalNewsToday, January 2023, accessed February 15, 2023, https://www.medicalnewstoday.com/articles/anxiety-and-brain-fog#other-causes-of-brain-fog.

The Prescription Ask

I consider myself a lucky woman. I only take one medication, a generic brand drug that will lower my cholesterol. On the unlucky side, because I am self-employed, my insurance is quite high and does not include a drug plan. The first time I ordered my low-cholesterol medication, it came to $41. That would last me three months. I thought this was a fair price and bought it. Just before I was about to run out of pills at the end of the third month, I went to the same pharmacy. This time, for a three-month supply, it was over $100. I spoke with the pharmacist, and she told me that the pharmacy does change generic suppliers from time to time. Not willing to fork out over $100, I went home and searched all my drawers for coupons and downloaded a few from some medical websites. I was pretty creative because I found coupons from GoodRx, AAA, and my NY State identification card that covered certain medications. I printed them all out and marched myself back to the pharmacy. I laid these crumpled-up pieces of paper with bar codes. The very sweet young man at the pharmacy counter scanned them one by one, and none applied. So I asked to speak with the pharmacist again, and this is what I said:

> The big lesson I learned here is this: even when you feel all the odds are stacked against you, especially when it comes to medicine and medications, it doesn't hurt to ask.

"You've been so helpful and patient, and I really appreciate it. I'm self-employed, my insurance does not have a drug plan, and I have tried to use every coupon possible, but none applies. The generic prices for low-cholesterol medications keep fluctuating, so is there something we can do to keep this price more consistent?"

She told me to give her some time, and she would see what she could do. I perused the cold and flu aisle. I had no idea there were so many types of cough syrup. She finally called me to the counter and said I was in luck. If I would be willing to come once a month and buy the pills at a thirty-day supply rather than a ninety-day supply, the prescription would be free. "Free?" I asked in a bit of disbelief. No drug is ever "free." She said, "Well, coding it this way, yes, it is free." I thanked her profusely and walked out of the pharmacy feeling a bit taller—even at five feet two—that together, the pharmacist and I championed one for the consumer and not Big Pharma!

The big lesson I learned here is this: even when you feel all the odds are stacked against you, especially when it comes to medicine and medications, it doesn't hurt to ask. Had I not asked, to this day, I would be paying a surprise amount every three months. Instead, I have zero surprise pricing, zero to pay, and zero trepidation when it comes time to purchase my pills.

The Insurance Ask

Have you ever made a doctor's appointment when you ask them on the phone if they take your insurance, they say yes, and then one month later, you get socked with a huge medical bill you thought would be covered by insurance? I have, plenty of times. In fact, I'm still battling between the doctor's office and my insurance company over a mammogram I had a year ago. My primary care doctor and her team practice under a leading university medical system here in NYC that my insurance company covers. My insurance covers a yearly mammogram. I went to one of the university's medical offices at 7:00 p.m. to get my approved mammogram, and the technicians had left. One of the doctors who was present said that she could do it for me because there was no sense in rescheduling my appointment. Since the doctor did the mammogram and not a technician, my visit was coded as a doctor's visit in a hospital, not a routine mammogram at an imaging center. It took me months to figure this out. In fact, the university medical system turned my claim over to a collection agency because I refused to pay.

When it comes to you and your medical insurance, I have several asks you can make that will save you the aggravation from making dozens of phone calls to straighten out your bill. It will also save you a ton of time. I draw upon all the time-consuming experiences I have had with these battles. First, when you call to make an appointment, do not say, "Does your medical practice 'take' this insurance?" I did that once with an eye, nose, and throat doctor. After my consultation with the doctor, the receptionist said, "Yes, we take your insurance, but consultations are not generally not covered with your type of insurance." Every word counts when you make an ask. Don't make my mistake and ask if they will "take" your insurance. Make sure your insurance company lists the doctor you want to see as an approved provider. Then call the doctor's office, let them know you contacted your carrier, and ask them, "Will my consultation be covered in full with this insurance?"

Next, master the coding game. Do a search on the code of the service you are contesting. I did mine on Google. That is where I discovered the code they used was for a doctor's visit at a hospital, not a mammogram at an imaging center. Once you have the facts, you craft your ask:

"I'm calling in refence to account number [your account number on the bill] on [date of your visit], and my date of birth is [your birth date]. The code number you assigned is [give them the code number], which is for a doctor visit at a hospital, when in reality I had a routine mammogram at your imagining center at [give the address]. Can you now go into my file, change the code, and remove this charge in your billing system?" Facts are your friends, so use them in your insurance asks.[14]

The Ask for Spirituality

A girls' weekend in the Catskills and afternoon facials and massages were well overdue. I went with my partner, who was celebrating a very big birthday, and her two sisters. One of her sisters, Carissa, had a big celebration as well. Earlier she had been diagnosed with stage 4 ovarian cancer. It was devastating news for all of us. Honestly, we all cried for many days, thinking her chances of survival were not very good, considering the late stage of her diagnosis. Carissa was determined that through her faith, her daily prayers to Saint Peregrine, and Father Michael McGivney—and her deep connection to her spirituality—she could beat this cancer. Also her driving force to live was that her two children were about to enter military academies and needed her.

It was a rainy, dreary day, the kind when you just want a warm blanket, some hot tea, and a good book or a good Netflix movie. We decided to wander the stores of Woodstock, New York. This town is famous for being the adjacent city to Bethel Woods, where the actual 1969 Woodstock concert was held. Yes, there are still more rainbow-colored peace signs in the most creative shapes and sizes than one can imagine throughout this entire town. We made our way into the Mirabai bookstore. We were in there a long time because Carissa wanted to smell every candle, touch every crystal, and buy healing presents for herself and her children. It was her happy place, one where she felt that to linger was to feel the essence of healing powers. After Carissa had made some purchases but still wanted to wander the bookstore, I decided to kill

---

14   For more examples and tips on health asks, see Laura Fredricks, *Money Wellness: Is Money Making You $ick?* (Indiana: Balboa Press, 2016).

some time by setting up a game for myself. Since there were stacks and stacks of books, I wanted to close my eyes and then look out and see which book cover would appeal to me the most. Since I was writing this book and the cover had not been decided yet, I thought I would get an idea of what would stand out so that in time, my book would stand out as well. I wanted my cover to be the one that would make people say, "What's this book about? I love the colors and the design!" or "The cover matches the title, and I need help with asking." I closed my eyes, opened them again, and there it was on a high bookcase, with a soft baby-blue-and-white cover with magnificent angel wings that just said: "Look at me, Laura." I knew it was the one. I picked it up, and the book was titled *Angels in Waiting: How to Reach Out to Your Guardian Angels and Spirit Guides*. I flipped the book open to a random page. It was page 22. Any number with two in it is my lucky number of choice. There on page 22 was a subchapter: "Reaching Out To Your Guardian Angel." It was all about asking, and here are some excerpts from that page:[15]

> When you ask for spiritual help, you have nothing to lose and everything to gain. Unwavering and powerful support is there for you. Just ask.

- "You have your own personal guardian angel, a being that has watched over you since you were born."
- "Asking in your mind for their help is all you need to do to engage their assistance."
- "The key word here is exactly that: ask."
- "You have to actively engage them by asking for their help."

---

15   Robbie Holtz and Judy Katz, *Angels in Waiting: How to Reach Out to Your Guardian Angels and Spirit Guides* (Rochester: Destiny Books 2021), 22.

I knew I wanted to add a section on asking for spirituality in this book, but I never thought I would get the inspiration by randomly picking up a book in a bookstore that had an attractive cover. There are truly no coincidences in this life.

Asking to be more spiritual is a hard ask. We are so busy, so consumed with day-to-day life, that spirituality can take a big back seat until we really need it, like when a tragedy occurs, when we feel lost and helpless, or when we experience deep pain or depression. No matter how often or when we need to ask for spirituality, we just need to ask for it. This ask is one you make to yourself, imploring the help of others you feel can heal and comfort you the most. It could be a person who is so admired in the religious sector, your guardian angel, a loved one who has passed, a shaman, a sage, or an advisor. When you ask for spiritualty, you are asking for guidance and placing your belief in something or someone that is greater and beyond yourself. Carissa asked St. Peregrine to heal her open-wound cancer, as he healed his open cancer wound on his leg. She prayed to Father McGivney because he was a beautified priest who founded the Knights of Columbus to help families stay together when the head of the household died. Her ask of him was to keep her alive so she could provide for her daughter and son. Her prayers and her spiritual ask worked. Against staggering medical odds, she beat it all, and to this date, she is cancer free.

When I am feeling overwhelmed and cannot think straight, I know that I have not set aside that quiet, meditative time, and that is what I need the most. So to be easy on myself, I begin my ask with expressing gratitude and say:

"I am so grateful to have set aside this peaceful time to be able to reach out to you for help. Right now I'm feeling so overwhelmed, and I know you can help me to quiet my mind and focus on something that is greater than myself. Can you guide me now how I can do this?"

Then I sit still just for a few minutes, taking larger breaths than I have all day, and my head feels lighter.

Have you ever had the experience that someone or something was telling you that a loved one was in great trouble or danger or may die? I was walking back from the home of a client I was coaching so that he could make some very large asks before he retired. He lives in my neighborhood, and just as I was about to pass my church, Our Lady of Pompeii in the West Village, I sensed that my mother couldn't breathe and might die. I have no idea where this thought came from, and it is not like me to randomly have these dark thoughts. I looked at my watch, and it was 11:15 a.m. This sense that something was about to happen was so strong that I had to know the exact time I was feeling it. I immediately entered the church, walked toward the altar, knelt down on the pew, and prayed:

"Please, dear God, do not take her now. We have just gotten to the place where we are enjoying each other in my adulthood, and I have too much that I need to learn and know from her. Can you give us more time together?"

That afternoon I called my mother, not wanting to share this because I thought it would scare her and put thoughts in her head that she may die soon. Before I got to my story, she said that she didn't want to scare me, but around 11:30 a.m. that morning, she had severe chest pains, the worst she had experienced in years. She couldn't breathe and almost fell on the kitchen floor. She made her way to the drawer where she kept her nitroglycerin pills and quickly swallowed one. She sat in her chair for an hour with her eyes open, fearing that if she closed them, she would die.

When you ask for spiritual help, you have nothing to lose and everything to gain. Unwavering and powerful support is there for you. Just ask.

The Ask for Trust and Forgiveness

Sophia; her husband, Blair; and their children were living very comfortably. Their children went to a private school, she had her own boutique designer clothing business, and he was a self-made entrepreneur focusing on investment opportunities for start-up clean energy companies. They belonged to a private club, and their children had private tennis lessons. All their money, retirement funds, investments, savings, and checking were in their joint names. Over time, Sophia started to notice that Blair was coming home from work with less spark and less enthusiasm and was more reserved. She always asked him how he was, and his answer was always the same: "We are working on something really big, and it is just a matter of time."

Blair always paid their bills on time, and this was one responsibility he took over and didn't mind doing. One day Sophia noticed a stack of bills on the desk that she thought Blair had paid. She thought in this instance, he had forgotten, was busy, or would get to it soon. Later that week, she received emails and text messages from the mortgage company, the credit card companies, and the utility company that the bills were overdue. Sophia went over to the unpaid stack of bills and flipped through them to see what had not been paid. The bill that shocked her the most was from their children's private school. Tuition was overdue—long overdue—and she knew this would jeopardize her children's continued placement at the school. When she confronted Blair to explain this bill as well as the others, Blair told her they all had been paid and there was some misunderstanding. Sophia said that she was starting with the tuition bill to get matters straight and would contact the school's head of finance to set up a meeting for the three of them. The morning of the meeting came, and Blair said he could not go because this deal that he had been working on for so long was about to come through. Sophia went to that meeting alone—not happily, but she went. She discovered that, yes, it was true: tuition had not been paid for quite some time, and she felt enormously embarrassed. She assured the financial officer at the school that she would go to the bank immediately and rectify the situation.

Sophia walked a few blocks to the bank that held their mortgage, checking, and savings. She sat with her bank's private client specialist and explained that she needed to make a direct transfer from their checking or savings account to the school to cover the tuition arrears. The private client specialist brought up their bank record on the computer to show Sophia the state of their bank accounts. Sophia felt as though she'd been punched in the stomach. There was nothing left in her accounts. It had been all withdrawn a week ago by her husband. Then the private client specialist started typing again on her computer. Sophia was hoping she had the wrong account pulled up. Worse news. There was an equity line of credit taken out by her husband against the money they paid toward the mortgage. Now 80 percent of what they paid toward the mortgage was in this line of credit to her husband.

Sophia, now outraged and filled with anger, asked her husband that night, "How could you ruin—destroy—our family financially?" Blair continued in his denial that he did anything wrong, and it was in the best interest of the family. He resented the question and just kept repeating, "We are on the brink of a really big deal."

After a few years had passed, Sophia and her husband separated. She felt that while they were a couple, he was off acting on his own and keeping Sophia in the dark. She felt that he never saw them as equals or partners, so it never occurred to him that he was acting behind Sophia's back. He was off doing his thing while she did hers, and sometimes their lives overlapped.

I share this scenario for many reasons. First, it is about money and the possible ruination of a couple and a family's financial stability. Second, it is about the dysfunction in a relationship in which one person can think that being a couple implies that all important decisions will always be made together, while the other is acting independently without any remorse. There is, however, a much more important element to this story. It's about trust. If you don't trust someone, what do you really have? Here, Sophia trusted Blair to take care of paying the bills as he had done in the past. Blair, in his own world, trusted Sophia to agree with him that what he was doing was in all their best interest because his "big deal" would be worth it in the end.

If you find yourself even near this situation, in the midst or at the tail end of a similar scenario, my ask to the person who has harmed you would be this:

"We have been together all these years, and I thought whenever we had a problem, we would work it out together. You taking out money from our accounts without even talking to me first is beyond hurt. You broke my trust in you. When did you so lose trust in us as a couple that you would do these things behind my back?"

I believe that anyone who knows or hopes that someone will ask for forgiveness must first get to the trust issue. Where and when did the trust break down? Blair could have easily asked Sophia to forgive him and say that he would never do it again, but would Sophia believe him enough, trust him enough to even consider his ask to be forgiven? If you feel someone needs to ask your forgiveness, and indeed they do ask for it in their own way, I strongly recommend you model your response with a question, as we did in the example with Sophia above. Depending on your satisfaction with the answer, that would be my gauge for you to determine whether or not you want to forgive this person.

Conversely, if you want to ask someone for forgiveness, I would definitely ask and solidify their trust in your ask:

"I know what I [did/said/didn't do/didn't say] upset you, and you have every right to be angry and disappointed. Your trust and your faith in me going forward is the most important thing to me. I'm asking you to forgive me. And please tell me: What can I do to earn back your trust in me?"

A forgiveness ask without a trust element contained in your ask will not get you very far. It may smooth things over for a while, but the person who is forgiving you may stay distant, sit back and watch your actions, and listen to you to before they totally and completely feel that you can be trusted. This is an incredibly hard ask to make and one that is often done poorly or not at all. The stakes are high because relationships can be broken and never mended, egos can take over, and "shoulds" come flooding in: "They should have known better," "I should never have trusted them," and "They should know I would never say that behind their back." Go easy on yourself if you need to make this ask—but do it. Make sure you ask not only to be forgiven but also to win back the person's trust in your ask so that you can all go forward.

When the Answer Is No

A "no" response is a killer. Who wants to hear "No"? It can feel like a gut punch, like someone ran over you or let out all the oxygen in the room. It doesn't have to feel that way if you remember these mantras:

- "No" now is not "Never later."
- "No" now is an invitation to keep in touch with them.
- "No" is an answer, one far better than never receiving a response.

We have just covered how to handle a lot of hard asks. If you do receive a no answer, I have a variety of ways you can handle it. First, your only job when you hear a no is to find out why. Why did they say no? Much like our follow up when you hear "I have to think about it," and your only job is to discover what the "it" is, as we covered earlier in the book, we also have to find out the rationale behind the no. Keep it simple and use similar words:

- "Thank you for letting me know. One thing that is important to me is to learn why you said no."
- "To the extent you feel comfortable with me, can you share with me why you said no [or turned down this opportunity]?"

Do not go into the assumption land of guessing why they said no. It will not serve you, your business, or your charity. Also, no comes in many forms. A doctor may tell you that you are not a candidate for this procedure. Instead of guessing that it is your age, your symptoms, your medical history, or immune system, ask your doctor: Why?

Second, once you know the reason that the person you ask articulated (and not you guessing), that is your invitation to stay in touch with them. The worst thing you can do is "take your no and go home." Instead say:

"Thank you for letting me know. I truly appreciate your honesty. I'd like us to stay in touch since we have both learned so much from each other. Is it OK with you if I call you from time to time?"

In all my years, I have never had someone say, "No, I really do not want to ever hear from you again." That's what it can sound like in your head when you hear no or when you think of asking them to stay in touch as I have presented to you. Think about it. This is a person who made your priority list to ask for something you need. Why would you take their initial no as a signal that they do not want to keep the relationship going?

As an alternative and a personal favorite of mine, I like to use a touch of humor coupled with a sincere delivery. I like to say: "Thank you so much. Life is long, and you never know where it will lead you. Can I circle back with you next May and see if we can work something out together?"

You can also use the word "revisit": "Can we revisit this—say, around next May—and see whether we can work this out together?"

I've won over more clients who initially said no to my consulting proposals and donors who said no to my initial philanthropic asks with this ask. It will work for you. You have my permission to borrow it!

Finally, if you just cannot find your way to try these responses, or it is just not your style to do so, think of this. You have a definitive answer. It is worse, far worse, not to receive an answer and go chasing after it with multiple follow-ups, eating away at your time, than to have your answer. They actually did you a favor. They responded. While the no answer is not ideal, if you say over and over a number of times, "No now is not a no forever," you will feel better about yourself, shake off this one occurrence, and get back to asking again. Don't let the "no"

> Don't let the "no" get to your head, your drive, your ambition, your psyche. You are far too good for that. Tackle the no and move on. Better things are on your horizon.

get to your head, your drive, your ambition, your psyche. You are far too good for that. Tackle the no and move on. Better things are on your horizon.

Now I do hope you feel stronger and more confident that you can tackle these hard asks and others with more ease. Since I'm a big hiker, I like to analogize it this way. When I'm ready to do a big hike, one that is known to be challenging with a lot of ice, steep scrambles, and no trail markers, I always have a bit of anxiety, coupled with a few swirling thoughts about my ability to do it and whether I really want to do this with my free time. Then I think I have my map and my GPS, which will guide me with each step. I just need to bring my positive attitude and my focus and get on with the hike. You now have the map and your GPS—the words to use when making your hard asks. Bring on your positive attitude with your focus, and you will have the winning combination to tackle and conquer any hard ask.

Takeaways

- Every ask should be two sentences and one question: 2S+1Q. This will prevent you from overasking your ask or making your ask too confusing for the person to make a decision.

- Asking for personal help: Recognize, acknowledge, and empathize with the person you are asking, explain why you need help, and then ask how you can solve it together.

- Asking for career help: Be sure to include a specific amount and when you want it. How they treat you when you ask for something is how you are going to be treated in this job.

- The ask is a conversation, not a confrontation: When you end your ask with a question, you are inviting more discussion, which keeps your ask alive.

- The ask for money: When you ask for money, you are not taking something away; you are giving an opportunity. For investment asks, be sure to ask people and entities in priority order.

- Getting your money back: Do not let time slip away; ask for the money back by a certain date as well as how you are to be paid. Always put any loan in writing with the terms of the loan, and ensure that both of you sign it.

- Asking for charity: People will give if they know, like, and trust you. When asking friends to support the charity you love, honesty wins the day, so let them know why you are asking them. If you do not ask them, they will feel there is a group richer, smarter, and better, and they are not in it.

- When planning your ask meeting, let the person know it is not just a coffee meeting.

- The ask formula works, regardless of the amount of the ask.

- Asking for health: Be proactive and come with a written list of questions for the doctor.

- Asking for medications: Ask the pharmacist if there is any alternative way to get your prescription cost lowered.

- Asking for insurance: Don't ask, "Will you take my insurance?" Ask, "What specifically will be covered under my insurance?"

- Asking for spirituality: Asks need to be specific, and remember you have the unwavering support from someone or something greater than yourself.

- Asking for trust and forgiveness: These two go together if you truly want to have someone's forgiveness. Ask for their trust in you and their forgiveness so you both can move forward.

- No now is not no forever: Keep your ask alive by staying in touch because life is long, and you never know when someone will circle back or revisit your opportunity.

CHAPTER 10

Let's Keep It Going

You've discovered that you have always had the ask in you since you were a child. You've learned how to tackle the really hard asks in your life, and now it is time to reflect back and see which part or parts of this book really resonated with you. Did the four asking types surprise you? Did you have any idea that with the right preparation, you would be organized, structured, and focused for any ask you make? Did Laura's Five Laws of Asking give you a new perspective regarding how your ask can be streamlined so that you'll receive an answer sooner than you thought possible? Finally, after reading how the right word selection, with the right tone, with the ask formula of "2S+1Q," will you find it easier to want to make the hard asks you may have tried to avoid making before?

I invite you now to hop on my website, www.ExpertOnTheAsk. com, and share your stories with me. What worked? What didn't? What came up unexpectedly? Each month I will be selecting from your stories the ones that are most successful as well as the ones that are most challenging. Your stories with my suggestions will be posted on my social media, so be sure to follow me. I will be doing short videos about your stories, so be sure to sign up on my mail list. I promise to keep it anonymous if you wish.

- All social media: ExpertOnTheAsk
- Website to post your stories and receive my videos: www. ExpertOnTheAsk.com

Just take a minute and think about this: Wouldn't it be great if more people knew how to ask? How much more relaxed, less stressed, less fatigued, and less complicated would your work environment and relationships be? This is why I highly encourage you, if you've picked up just one or two (hopefully more) ideas and action steps that you feel will help you ask better and that you can do immediately, to share this book with your friends, loved ones, people at work, and people you volunteer with—the people you enjoy.

There will always be a new situation, a new predicament, a new challenge that needs the right ask, and I stand ready to help you.

The quality of your life depends on the quality of the questions you ask yourself and others. My money's on you.

Printed in the USA
CPSIA information can be obtained
at www.ICGtesting.com
JSHW021504060524
62631JS00004B/43